A Beautiful Lie

By: K.D. Laymon

"Keenan Laymon tells his personal story of being raised in a Christian home, with loving parents, but losing his way as a teen. His narrative is not for the faint-of-heart, with his raw, honest report of how far he strayed before finding his way back to God again. I'm sure his book will help **turn other prodigals around,** and **bring hope** to parents as well."

Pastor Jerry McQuay,
Christian Life Center

"Keenan Laymon gives an account of his miraculous deliverance from debilitating drugs and the powers of evil. **All need to hear and heed his message.** His work gives a clear path of deliverance from a hopeless life to a life worth living and immeasurable joy that we all seek and for which we were created."

James B. Shelton, PhD
Professor of New Testament
Oral Roberts University

"Keenan is the real deal. His story is a dramatic example of the **life changing power of God.** If you or a loved one are struggling with the destructive power of drugs, especially psychedelic drugs, **this true story could change your life!**"

Pastor Gary Mauro,
Calvary Chapel Sawgrass

"I would encourage anyone who has questions about the reality of Jesus, **read this powerful testimony of God's grace**. If you know someone who questions the reality of Jesus, **get this book in their hands**."

Pastor Mike Fehlauer,
New Life Church

Contents

A note from the Author

Herein lies my testimony—my recollection of true historical events as I lived them—no exaggerations. I prayed as I prepared these words and also asked that all co-laborers do the same in order that this, my story of God's pursuit of me, might build the kingdom of God.
Names are changed to protect confidentiality.

—Keenan Laymon

Intro

In Medias Res

As I looked into the demon's eyes, my legs quivered. I felt as though my feet had railroad spikes hammered through them into the ground. I tried to look left and right, but my gaze was always pulled back into its eyes. I feared looking away as much as a feared looking head on, but I couldn't pull myself away. I began to believe all that had been told to me up to that point, the hopelessness and feeling of abandonment grew within my soul. I knew there was only one way out of that situation, the way I was told, the way of suicide. I contemplated on how to go about doing it, where I could go, who I should tell. I was sure it was the only way out. I had no other form of escape. The demon spoke up and confirmed my thoughts by verbalizing them, "Suicide is the only way," it spoke.

Just as I had accepted what must be done, I heard another voice, "Go back!" it said. "This is nothing but a drug. In the morning, the sun will rise again." I felt the long nails that had been driven into my feet come out. I shifted my gaze to the side, turning my back on who stood before me, listening to the voice that overcame my own thoughts, the one that told me to go back. As I turned, I felt as though I had turned my back on a prowling lion waiting for its opportunity to strike. I began taking steps, with each one feeling as if it carried an extra 200 pounds. "You'll never forget! *We* will always be there!" I heard the demon screech from behind me…

Back to the Beginning

Everyone's life starts out with innocence, and so did mine. But my choices led to terrifying events that changed the course of my future. What you've just read is only the tip of the iceberg.

This is my testimony. It illustrates the devil's maneuvers and methods. I can look back at each event in my life and see the evil force pulling me deeper and deeper into my destruction. But, at the time, I couldn't see it.

I start from the beginning, so these attacks that beckoned me to hell on earth can be seen.

While reading, keep this in mind: whether or not you believe in God; God and the Devil are in a struggle over each individual's life. We see it if we have eyes to. I pray that everyone who reads this understands and sees the absolute truth that is God. Amen.

Part I
Growing Up Laymon

Introduction

If you ever want to understand the reason a person thinks or acts the way they do, ask about their upbringing. Many things contribute to the way a person behaves, such as a life changing event, a word of encouragement at the right moment, a parental figure, the list goes on. I have included these select informational paragraphs on my upbringing, in order that my worldview becomes more understandable as the story progresses. If you read closely enough, you will discover many hints of what will come of my future, as if someone was warning or preparing me from a young age. My childhood displays early signs of distrust for the world and my mother, a love for manipulation and strategy, a desire for money, and an "I can do it myself" attitude, all of which play vital roles within my life.

Getting Started

I grew up on the south side of Chicago in a little town called Homewood, Cook County. It was a beautiful town filled with wonder and excitement. I lived on Sycamore Street with my two parents, one brother and two sisters—all two years apart. Both sisters are older than us boys, and my brother is two years younger. So, it goes Michall as the first born, Moriah, me, then Garrett.

Our childhood was pretty normal. Our parents were strict and just but they wielded a merciful hand—Christians, which, for us, meant no *Simpsons*, no *Harry Potter* witchery, no Pokémon or Yu-Gi-Oh. And, any movies that had creatures besides humans—out. Death? Out. Curse words—that's what the mute button was for. As such, I never heard a curse word until second grade. PG-13 movies weren't allowed until my fourteenth year, and so on.

We spent a lot of time locked out of the house. "You don't need to be inside all day," our mom would say, so we'd go to friends' houses and play video games. South Chicago was a wonderful place to grow up, complete with a ballpark in my backyard and a playground down the street that always brought new friends. Down the street we had a local pool that everyone hit up in the summertime. And Dairy Queen ... oh, Dairy Queen! The street I lived on was quiet and had other kids my age. We played capture the flag, ghost in the graveyard, etc. Or, the neighborhood kids would come over for trampoline dodgeball until the sun went down and the dark night sky twinkled overhead. Our street was calm, but violence lurked just ten miles down the road. Violence didn't really touch us directly, but I learned early to grab the candy bar from the *back*, because the front ones had bites out of them. I was all about getting the most out of my money.

I cared more about money than sports. I sold lemonade, baseball cards, basketball cards ... I even painted a smiley face on a rock to sell it to the 3-year old across the street. One day, I set up a gambling booth. Now, *that's* where the money was at. Kids all over the block ran down the street to buy their chance to win a Hot Wheels car.

The gig was this: one dollar per game (although, I bought Hot Wheels at the store for $0.50 a piece). The contender selected one of eight cars from a table. The house picked after. The two were launched from a Hot Wheels toy launcher, and the car that went the farthest won—simple. If you win, you keep the car. And, these were sweet-looking wheels. Of course, there was a trick. The launcher had a button. We'd press the button for the house, but we'd throw in a little whiplash action, which gave our car an extra boost. I pulled about $50 dollars from that street stand.

I can remember as a child, lying in my bed at night with my brother sleeping next to me in his bed. I was always so thankful for a brother to sleep next to me in my room. I figure he always thought that if someone was going to break into our house, I would protect him; but, I always went to sleep comforted that he would protect me. Every night we prayed for God to come into our hearts and keep us strong in our lives and make sure that we would ultimately rest in Heaven with him. At that time, I really didn't understand I had a choice in whether or not I wanted to believe in God, it was simply something I had grown up with. We went to Sunday school and church without fail—every Sunday plus Christian bonus points for attending each Wednesday, too. This went on roughly until I was 14 or 15.

When I would sleep as a child, I can recall a dream I would have every night for more than a year—perhaps a better word is nightmare:

In it, I would be sitting in a red-hot Camaro with my mom driving. She would slowly come to a stop in front of an unmarked building, park the car, and leave me in it while she went inside. I would unbuckle my seatbelt and slide over to the driver's side, sitting comfortably behind the steering wheel. I would try to start the car and give it some gas, but every time it rolled backwards, and I'd scream for my mother to save me.

Then, I'd wake up in a cold sweat. I never thought anything of the dream itself but looking back, it seems meaningful. As children, our parents tend to steer the direction of our lives but there comes a time that we slide ourselves behind the steering wheel of life. Maybe this dream was a fear I had at a young age of getting behind that wheel, or maybe it was a prophesy of what was to come. Either way, this dream gave me a lot of fear as a child, as did other things.

When I was young, I was terrified of the dark, and I'm convinced it's due to our basement's unfinished room. And I mean, *unfinished*—no light at all. In fact, one of the walls wasn't even plastered. I could see into the adjacent, room that was just as dark, through the wooden studs. Both rooms were packed with random things, some of which we didn't know the names of. My best friend and I challenged each other to see how long we could stay in there, taking steps further and further into the darkness. With each step becoming heavier and heavier as fear overtook the imagination of what laid behind every cardboard box, every random item stuffed onto the shelves. As our steps took us further into the darkness, our eyes could make out less and less of what waited before us. I remember getting as far as a wad of black string that resembled the top of some monster's head of hair. With adrenaline pulsing, we both would run out screaming, "The black hair!" every time.

As kids, our imaginations were unstoppable. We played made up games like crazy chicken, tennis ball tag, or cops and robbers all throughout the night. We even assembled a track in our house for our Hot Wheels which seemed to go on for miles. It was made up of a list of things we found around the house, like toilet paper roles, cardboard, and construction paper—not having enough track didn't matter. If we had the will, we would find the way.

One day, I found some wood and built my own go cart – minus the motor. To me, it was like a math problem that needed a solution. I measured and figured and solved it out piece by piece. I've always loved math and analysis in general. I'm a strategist at heart. I started studying battle tactics when I was eight years old. It was my passion and hobby and I had other hobbies as well. I was also a bit of an artist. My mom's an artist, so I get that from her. Even from a young age, she wouldn't let me scribble. "Stay in the lines," she'd say. As a result, it wasn't long before I was making art freehand out of my *Warhammer 40,000* book, drawing warriors of the future.

Part II
To Texas

Elementary School

School in south Chicago was an adventure—especially the bus. Kids were smoking and cussing left and right, and while this wasn't ultimately the reason we left Chicago for Texas, I'm sure it helped. My father's office shut down in Chicago, and they offered him a new job in Austin, Texas. Originally, we planned to live in New Braunfels, but we ended up a little north of Austin in a town called Cedar Park. The newness was exciting. I expected cowboys and ten-gallon hats, but we didn't see much of that. Our house was big, and the neighborhoods were spread out; it was a five-mile drive *minimum* to see a friend. Neighbors pretty much kept to themselves, which meant fewer options for friends. My parents thought that a couple of weeks of school there would get us a few friends before summer—it didn't.

In school, I was a jerk and I was a nerd. I didn't like seeing people getting bullied, so on the first day in fifth grade of attending my new school, my introduction to the class was shoving a giant kid off of a little guy during recess. No one had stood up to this kid before, "Pick on someone your own size!" I said while getting as close to his face as I could (he was a foot and a half taller than me). He walked away. Day one.

The next day, we sat around the teacher as she read a book to the class. It seemed immature to me. After all, Chicago considered fifth grade to be middle school, so naturally I felt like everything in my new school was a little to "kid-ish." The teacher finished reading and opened the floor for questions. The kid beside me shouted questions right in my ear, so I turned and shouted, "Shut the hell up!" That put me in the principal's office in about seven seconds. Day two.

Middle School

Soon enough, middle school rolled around. In middle school, I made a good number of friends. One friend in particular was Dean. Dean was the kid that constantly talked about people behind their backs. He never knew when to keep his mouth shut, and most people hated him, but he was my friend. He'd get picked on or beat up almost daily. A boy named Christian had it out for Dean from day one. He used to make Dean cry on the bus every day on the way home by doing different things to him. One day he grabbed him by the neck and slam his head into the bus window. I was surprised the window didn't crack. It was horrible to witness. Soon after that, I did what I thought had to be done—I brought a knife to school. I planned to stab Christian if he tried anything that day. I told someone about my plan, and the story made the rounds. As a result, I ended up in In-School Suspension (ISS). Believe it or not, by the end of eighth grade, I had kicked Dean's butt myself on several occasions. He had the nerve to talk about *me*. Some people never change.

Deciding Factors

Sometimes one single factor makes all the difference in a person's path, which is why I beat up Dean. I thought a few punches to his face would make him a better human. Some people need loss, pain, frustration, agony, defeat, love, or even loneliness to learn certain lessons in life. And I thought I was the one who needed to teach the lessons.

Others have an effect on us. It's important to actually choose the people who shape us because ultimately, they do.

Texas Means Football, but not for Everyone.

Every boy in my school was raised to play football. No lie; Texans are nuts about it. If, God forbid, a kid doesn't play football, then it's basketball, track or wrestling. I found the push of a sport on a young mind annoying and manipulative—the kids were completely brainwashed about the importance and necessity of it. Maybe that's why I separated myself from that world. Witnessing the way people grow up and act under different circumstances made me question my own upbringing. *Maybe I had been brainwashed?* I began to question at this age (12 years old). *Am I just a product of my own conditioning?* This question began to rattle around in my mind. It made me question a lot of things, including the foundational belief that I was raised with–that there is a God.

I only had a few friends, but we all had one thing in common: we didn't care about what others thought of us. We wore ridiculous outfits simply because we could. We stayed as far away as possible from the middle school drama.

In eighth grade, I started skating because I thought it was unique. It was my break away from the masses. None of my friends skated with me, but it's what I enjoyed doing in my downtime, and it slowly became a bigger and bigger part of my life.

My friends made up a decent airsoft team, and that was how we usually spent our time. My passion for military strategy pulled me into the position of team leader. I knew how to lead men, when to hold ground and when to take ground. One day, our team of six took on a team of more than twenty, and we only lost one man—we massacred the opposing team. After that, no one played against us. We had become too good.

Temptation Elevated

Between eighth and ninth grade, my parents put me into a church retreat called Elevate. The program included a four- or five-day stay in a resort. There must have been 500+ kids there.

At the resort, we had three-hour sermons in the morning and afternoon. They were intense. Kids broke down crying from witnessing the glory of the Lord.

In between sermons, we explored the resort. We swam or relaxed in the cabin with our teams that were assigned at the beginning of the trip. We collected points as a team by working together and won prizes at the end of the retreat.

There was a girl in my group who was probably the most beautiful thing I'd ever seen. Her name was Mary, but I didn't consider myself on level with Mary; I was covered in acne and felt generally hideous when it came to the opposite sex. I had no intention to talk to this girl, let alone become friends, but somehow, she liked me. I ignored her for the first three days of the retreat, but she kept flirting.

One day, Mary, and a couple friends and I, were sitting and talking on some rocks overlooking the camp's lake. That's when I found out Mary smoked weed and drank alcohol. She listened to dark music full of killing and hate, and I had no clue that kind of music even existed. As a teen, music meant a lot to me; I believed that it practically defined a person. At one point, Mary was all up in my space trying to get me to kiss her. Now, honestly, I went to camp to meet God not a girlfriend, but this girl had me wanting... I leaned in and kissed her. My life and story are both all downhill from here, the place where I first picked physical satisfaction over God.

Mary was on me the rest of the retreat, we held hands all the time, and the leaders had to separate us during services. "Just because we're in this haven doesn't mean the devil can't get to you," one of the leaders warned. "Get rid of the distractions and focus on God. The devil has many ways to throw you off the path of righteousness," he said. Even today, I remember it word for word, and even as that leader spoke, I was just thinking about Mary.

Praise and worship at Elevate was overwhelming, but to me it was manufactured. *Is this feeling actually God's presence or just an overly emotional atmosphere produced by long piano chords?* The room was full of emotion, and all my peers were falling to their knees—kids I never would have expected to do so. Some of them were even crying. Suddenly, a vision invaded my mind out of nowhere. It whisked me away to another place, a vision over sight that is for me and will not be recorded in this book. The Lord showed me who He had called me to be, and I didn't want anything to do with it. I pretended to have never seen the vision, but I knew what I saw. No 14-year old could play it cool after that, but I had the strongest of all distractions: Mary.

My beautiful distraction and I hung out the rest of the retreat. I was completely infatuated. I was sure it was love. Maybe it was. And when the retreat was over, I hoped to stay in touch.

When I had gotten back home, I decided I would make up a persona to match hers—one where I smoked and drank like her, one where I had a list of favorite rappers. We laughed about how funny it would be to smoke weed in an Above the Influence jacket. I transformed myself—for her.

I got her number and texted her nonstop. A week later, she agreed to be my girlfriend. Her city, Pflugerville, was a 30-minute drive from me, so we only saw each other on Sundays at the church our parents brought us to. From then on, it was as if the Sunday sermons didn't exist. I didn't even notice them—not with Mary by my side. We'd sit in the risers and talk through the whole thing. She was always high. My transformation into a different person continued. I stole money from my parents (a first for me), and I bought her that Above the Influence jacket.

Soon thereafter, Mary stopped texting back. I heard through the grapevine that she had a boyfriend at her school. Turned out to be true. I saw a picture of him through mutual friends at the church, and he looked just like me. Apparently, they'd been a couple before the retreat and had broken up when I met her. That's why she came on so strong. Realizing I had been used as a rebound was devastating. Everything I thought about myself—that I was unlikeable, ugly, stupid, on a lower level—well, those thoughts must be true. Within weeks, I'd wrapped up my entire identity in her. *What an idiot I am,* I thought. I plunged into a deep depression.

I blamed everything on my family's move to Texas. I thought to myself, T*his never would have happened in Chicago.* Then, I threaten to kill myself to try to get Mary to talk to me again. She wouldn't. I thank God I didn't do something stupid and actually go through with it.

I moved on to other girls, but only ones who reminded me of Mary. I'd rush things or tell ridiculous lies to get girls to pity me. Meanwhile, I kept asking God if He was real. "You keep watching me suffer even though I'm asking you to show Yourself," I would cry out to the sky. My parents noticed that I had fallen into a depression though they didn't know where it had come from. They decided that it would be best for me to see a counselor since I had stopped telling them my problems and what had been going on in my life. About six months of counseling lifted me out of depression, but not before I told the Lord I was done with Him. While I was depressed, I would cry out to God asking him to show me if he was real... Never did I get an answer.

One night, I couldn't go to sleep. I walked out onto the back porch at 2:00 am completely fed up with God. I made this vow. "Lord I have asked and asked for you to show me yourself and still you watch me suffer. So I'm leaving you now, if I was ever even with you, because I bet the devil will show me a demon before you show me your face."

Talk about foreshadowing.

The Descent

About ten characters are introduced within this book that had significant impact on my life. Though there were many others, the people that will be introduced through side notes in the following section, are crucial. Some of them I met at the skatepark, others through drugs, and some I still don't know how they came into my life. In retrospect, I realize each friendship represents another level of descent, another footstep into that dark room that my friend and I would dare each other to go into as a child. Closer and closer, we would be drawn to that wad of black string that made us run out screaming "the black hair!" However, at the end of this, it would not be a ball of black string that made me run out of the darkness, but something much more sinister.

High School

I hung out with my old friends in high school, and the lies I started telling Mary I was still telling all my peers. I said I smoked a lot of pot and got screwed up at parties, but I had still never been high. My middle school friends were slowly fading away. Then, one day, Mark moved to town.

The Back Story on Mark

Mark was a scrappy kid that had moved from another part of Texas. He loved to skateboard, like me, which is why we started to grow closer to one another. Some days, we would skate until two in the morning. Mark lived a block from the school, and he always had a fridge full of drinks and a pantry full of food. Needless to say, I was always going over to his house. We did everything together and became best friends very quickly.

Mark and I had classes together, and I raved to him about pot like I did to everyone else. He said he had never smoked but was curious about it. Mark was a momma's boy. That kid's mom would do *anything* for him. And, if she wouldn't, just give her 15 minutes to change her mind. Marks demands ran her credit card debt through the roof. Mark would even have her take us to the skatepark only to turn around and pick us up because we didn't like whoever happened to be there on several occasions. He'd break a board and she'd buy him a new one the same day. It was astonishing and also made me pretty jealous. I never had that kind of attention.

The Back Story on Jory

Mark had an older brother named Jory by a different dad—one who beat Jory and his mom pretty bad until he died when Mark was 4 and Jory was 11. Jory huffed, smoked meth, drank and basically got screwed up on anything he could get his hands on. He bought us alcohol; there was no one cooler. I looked up to him.

I figured Mark's mom treated Mark so well so he wouldn't turn out to be like Jory. Mark never wanted to be like Jory, but I did. I fueled Mark's desires to want to smoke weed and do drugs every chance I could.

I didn't want to be like Dean, the drama kid from my middle school days. I wanted to live the kind of lifestyle that someone like Mary would want. I was done being a nerd, and I couldn't tolerate my family anymore. I'd blamed them for so long about our move to Texas because I thought it was so selfish that my parents wanted to be near their parents. *Why couldn't they go to Florida where my dad's side lives with all of our cousins?* I thought. That blame turned to resentment and filled my heart with nothing but bitterness toward my parents, my mother particularly.

I thought of myself as pretty mature and hated that my mom didn't realize that. She babied me with strict rules, but I rebelled against every one. She overprotected me to the point where I just stopped talking to her. *What's the point?* I thought. *It's either "back-talk" or "sarcasm."* I felt like a slave. "Why don't we talk?" she would ask. Then, I'd unleash with a list of her faults.

My animosity toward my mother only made Mark's mom look like a more perfect parent. *Why isn't my mom like this?* I wondered. I wanted to be listened to and have conversations without being wrong, I wanted a little freedom.

My mom made friends with every one of my friend's parents. Ultimately, my mom became friends with Mark's mom, which caused his mom to start acting a little differently—more like my mom. Yeah ... he didn't like that. He started calling my mom horrible names and telling me how crazy and overbearing she was. "She wants you in a box of rules," he said. Of course, I couldn't argue with him. I thought it was true.

Eventually, I turned away from my parents completely. I stayed away from home as much as possible at places where I could do and say what I wanted.

Mark and Me

Together, Mark and I began to smoke weed (without him knowing I had never smoked a day before in my life). I told him I was a pro at this. Jory supplied us, so getting our hands on weed was super easy. We smoked cigarettes as well, mostly because all the other skaters did, but also because it was relaxing after a loaded pipe (bowl) of weed. We became inseparable, skating everywhere, sometimes skating ten miles to find the perfect skate spot. He'd been skating already for four years, but I was just beginning to get seriously into it. I started learning tricks and got good quickly. On the weekends, we'd play video games and smoke—seemed fine to us.

Mark always talked about landing a skating sponsorship so he could go pro. The pros we saw on videos seemed so carefree. They never had to "grow up" and get a job, they got to spend their entire lives skating. I wanted to be like that, to never grow up or die trying. I didn't want the responsibility. I wanted the paycheck, but not the nine-to-five. I wanted fame and money, and I wanted it by the time I graduated high school. That's why eventually, I started my own shirt/skate company, and later, I joined a metal band as a screamer. *One of these things will make me my millions and cover me for the future,* I thought.

In reality, I was screwed.

Arrested

It wasn't long in our smoking careers that Mark and I got caught. The police sent me to jail for a night. On a separate occasion but within the same week, Mark got caught selling drugs for his brother, Jory. Our parents kept us from seeing each other, and we were both put on probation.

After all this, my family looked at me differently. It had only been two or three months of smoking weed, but my family wouldn't let me live it down. My sister called me a pothead and a mistake. I felt rejected. *You want a pothead?* I thought, *I'll give you a pothead.*

My Two Places

During probation, my parents let me go to band practice and the skatepark—I guess to be social and get exercise. Little did they know, that wasn't a great plan on their part.

My metal band practiced three times a week at our drummer's house. We were decent, but we all wanted this band to bring in money, so we took it very seriously. Austin is called the music capital of the world, so our chances seemed good. Not to mention that our guitarist was a prodigy and the rest the band wasn't bad either. We actually played big venues and headlined shows. But, after more than 50 shows, we hadn't brought in even $100.

The skatepark had to be the worst place I could have gone. The skatepark is where I bought drugs. As soon as I was off of probation, I smoked all the time. Mark and I never really reconnected. He dove into the party scene, and all those kids kept getting busted. I, on the other hand, was lucky enough to meet a kid named Jax.

The Back Story on Jax

I met Jax at the skatepark. He was a good guy and an even better skater. What's more, he smoked weed, *a lot.* The first time I met him, he was at the park with a cigarette in his mouth, and his eyes were blood shot red—he was high. As I got to know him, I found that he believed everything was better when you were high— skating, food, sleeping, sex, everything. His skating skills backed up his beliefs, so I decided to follow in his footsteps. I began to smoke weed and skate with Jax every day. Slowly but surely, I lost all ambition to learn new tricks and push myself.

Jax and I stayed out of the way of the police and stuck with smoking weed. When my grounding was lifted, my dad let me borrow his car every night. Jax and I would use it to buy and help sell weed. For months, we were high every night. Neither of us had a job, but we'd trade things with our dealer and beg. Multiple times we'd straight up find weed on the ground, *almost as if someone was taking care of us.* Nothing was fun without weed, but the weed was flowing, so life seemed good.

After a few months of just Jax and I getting high every day, Jax had to go back to Houston to live with his dad. Before he left, he introduced me to a kid named Ben, another skater. To this day, I've never seen anyone smoke more weed than Ben. He sold weed to fund all of his costly smoking.

The Back Story on Ben, Matt and David

Ben had two brothers (Matt and David) all of whom skated. David was older and had a kid, Matt was younger and eager to be like his brothers. All three of them shared a two-bedroom apartment that was pretty much dedicated to smoking and gaming. They lived with their parents who didn't seem to mind the constant weed smoking. From my perspective, weed was everything to these three brothers, and they seemed to be doing fine. I decided, I too wanted my life to revolve around this one thing, getting high. What was left of my ambition at this point had shifted toward another goal, living the high life.

At first, Ben and I skated together and then would play video games at his family's apartment. I stayed the night a few times and got stoned out of my mind. This cycle went on for a few months. They had weed, I had a desire to smoke it. That was the extent of our relationship. They would get me high for free, but whenever I had money, I would pay them. Plus, I would bring new customers to them that I met at the skatepark. It was a win-win situation.

I started my company I mentioned before around this time called "Why Not." I poured $300 into it, but I never really launched it. My ambition had dropped too low. Outside of skating and weed, nothing existed. Soon, even my skating plateaued. I completely stopped improving. I stopped learning new tricks and preferred to sit down at the skate park rather than skate. Then, my band ties disintegrated. We had the best times and knew we were destined for greatness, but my drug addictions lead me to spend less time with the band and more time with other people. Pretty soon, my already small world shrunk down again. It was just weed and me.

Another Girl

My world was good with weed, but then a girl came along—no names. She was a groupie that hung around our band. She'd slept with everyone in the band except me, but she talked to me online. She described everything we could do together, and one night, we did. She texted me at my drummer's house and said she was a few houses down with no parents. We slept together that night.

Later, she found out she was pregnant. I thought it was mine, but she'd slept with three other guys the same week, so there was no telling. I had no intention of letting my parents find out either way, which prompted me to scrounge together $500 for an abortion. I needed to make money quick. Fortunately for me I had been making money since I was a kid, ripping off the other neighborhood kids through my gambling stand and selling anything I could get my hands on. I had a lot of selling experience and I was good at it. So, I decided to do what Ben does, sell weed. For that, I would need my friend Trevor.

Easy Money with the Devil

Trevor was a raver (*someone who gets high to electronic music*), and he loved to snort molly (*ecstasy, a drug that induces euphoric effects, causing unreasonable happiness*) and take roles (*ecstasy/molly laced with amphetamines, heroin or acid*). He tripped (*hallucinated*) on acid (*a chemical that induces a hallucination*) and shrooms (*natural mushrooms that also induce hallucinations*); basically, Trevor did any and every drug except meth.

The Back Story on Trevor

Trevor was a dealer and a good friend that I had met in high school. We had gym together and would sneak off when the coach wasn't looking to go smoke weed in the woods. My other friends didn't like him. He did stupid things, but he was smart about how he did them, if that makes sense. He treated me well and even tried to help me quit smoking cigarettes. He loved doing drugs, and he sold the best drugs no matter what kind of drug it was.

Our weed was better than anyone else's, but we couldn't always get our hands on it, so we'd sell other drugs instead, like ecstasy, shrooms, acid, or cocaine. For a few months, we were the exclusive ecstasy supplier of the entire north side of Austin.

Trevor was a natural salesman, and he was good at getting people to try new drugs—that was his thing. He took "no" as a personal insult. I could see he was a manipulator. I kind of started to see him as a devil. One day, his hair stood up on both sides of his head like horns. I said, "Trevor, you're the devil." He laughed and changed the subject.

One time, Trevor sneezed, and I said, "God bless you." Then, he kept sneezing. I kept saying, "God bless you," and this continued for more than two minutes of continuous sneezes. When I didn't say God bless you, he stopped sneezing. That freaked me out. I declined the night's drug and texted a friend to pick me up. When the person called me back, Trevor snapped. He stood over me with his hand heavy on my shoulder and said, "You're not going anywhere. Stay here with me. Your friend is a loser. Take this molly with me." I looked up at him, and his hair stood up like horns again. I agreed to stay so he would settle down.

Six weeks of drug dealing made enough money for the abortion. When I delivered the money, the girl said she was already too attached to the child.

"I'm not fathering this kid," I said. I told her how lucky she was that I would even try to provide for the abortion. She wouldn't change her mind. She wouldn't take the money. She wouldn't get the abortion.

That didn't stop me. I barraged her every day until one day she told me she had had a miscarriage. It was the happiest day of my life. I suddenly had $500 dollars to spend as I pleased. I spent it all in three days—mostly on drugs.

Later, I found out the miscarriage story was a lie to get me to leave her alone. She planned to keep the child. On my birthday, the child was born. Years later, I tried to get into the child's life. I think deep down she knew I would, despite my claims. In 2015, when the child was five years old, a DNA test determined the baby wasn't mine.

No one knew any of this—not even Mark who was still one of my best friends. I never trusted people with secrets.

Old Times—Take *Two*

With the baby thing settled, I left Trevor for a while and went back to Ben, the guy who lived with his two other brothers and would get me high all the time. Jax moved back from Houston by that time, and Mark stopped partying and joined us along with a few others. We had a tight group of friends built on drugs and doing life together. We only really did one of two things: smoke at Ben's or skate. I had become very prideful at this point because of all the drugs that I had been doing with Trevor—the acid, shrooms, ecstasy, and even some drugs that I still can't remember. I didn't show it, but I felt better than all of them because I'd done hard drugs.

We started to go to Mark's place because he had a pool table, ping-pong table, Xbox, skate rails, internet, cable, and we could even smoke on the porch. His mom didn't say anything. She'd yell sometimes, but there was kind of an understanding that she had to do that even though she knew we wouldn't take it seriously.

The Wreck

One night, we all stayed at Mark's and then heard about a party going on that night. When the time came, only Jax and I left to go to the party. At the party, we got completely wasted and headed back to Mark's. Like all drunk drivers, I thought I was a good one. On the way back, Jax broke out a pack of cigarettes half a mile from Mark's house. He had stolen them at the party. I thought we were out of cigarettes, I was stoked. I decided at the last second to go drifting in the rear parking lot of a nearby school in celebration. I didn't make the first turn. I crashed into the curb, totaling my dad's car. The airbags deployed, and Jax bolted to Mark's house. I stayed to wait for the police.

When the police arrived, I pretended to be in a fragile state, yelling and pacing so they wouldn't get near enough to smell my breath. I kept it up until they allowed me to leave with my dad in his minivan who woke up at 3am to come get me. It worked. I got away without a DWI, but I was in trouble with my parents.

My parents grounded me from everything except the skatepark—once again, this was not a good idea on their part, considering all my friends and drugs came from the skatepark. No one would give me a ride, so I had to skate there myself. Mark called me a dumbass from then on and convinced my friend Ben that I was a loser. Ben fell off the map after that; he wouldn't even sell to me. Mark kind of took over that friendship and everything else I'd had, and it got to my head. Turns out, Jax had just been using me for my car, so he dropped out too, once the car was gone.

There I was, alone again, and deeper I plunged into a world of darkness.

Eventually, the grounding from my parents lifted, and I started hanging out with this young guy named Sky. Sky was the only one that would talk to me at the skatepark. He was all drama and a thief. Everyone hated him, but I thought I could teach him some life lessons—steer him toward a better path. Blind leading the blind.

The Back Story on Sky

Sky was a brother of a friend from the skatepark. No one wanted anything to do with Sky, not even his brother. Sky was a common criminal and was dumb about the way he went about doing things. He would get caught for the pettiest of crimes. Everyone knew that if you were going to hang out with Sky, you were going to get arrested. But, to be honest, my options for friends became very limited after the accident. There was no one else.

My friendship with him sealed my excommunication from everyone else. I gave Sky help and advice, and he looked up to me. He had no father, and his mom was a bipolar cocaine addict. He had a hair-trigger temper and got pissed at the most random stuff. He was kicked out of his home at 17 and dropped out of high school. He got his GED, but he had no money for college.

I couldn't imagine that kind of life—so hopeless. But, Sky wasn't depressed. In fact, his spirits were always up somehow. Even when his mom moved to Montana to get away from him, he pressed on. I liked that about him, so I'd give him money when I could, and I'd smoke all my weed with him. Our friendship lasted a few months.

Eventually, Sky got caught stealing from cars. The judge sent him off to military school for eight months.

Back at It

Literally the day after Sky left, I ran into Jax at the skatepark. His new friend, Creed, was with him, and I could never forget Creed after what happened in high school.

The Back Story on Creed

It was Freshman year. The fire alarm went off, and we were all outside waiting for the all-clear. I was off by myself in my JROTC (*Jr Officers' Training Corps*) uniform with a bowl-cut that my mother forced on me. I knew I looked like a dork, so I kept a knife in my pocket. Out of nowhere, Creed shoved me to the ground. My hand was already on my knife, so I flicked it open on the way down. Creed ran away, and I put the knife back into my pocket. He never screwed with me again.

Now, here was Creed at the skatepark with Jax whom I hadn't talked to since my car accident. Jax told me they'd been smoking a gram per day for the last two months, and that was enough reason for me to want to tag along. I joined up with them for the next eight months. Once more, finding weed became our life's purpose.

Every day, we'd do the same skate tricks then find some weed. We'd pawn stuff and trade our boards, anything that would get us some quick cash. We always drove on empty hoping there would be enough gas to get us to our dealer's house. We were proud of our way of life. Nothing mattered except getting high.

We were ignorant, and it was bliss, but it also brought its problems. For one, we had no food most days. We were desperate for cigarettes, so we all became mooches (*people that use others for resources*). We'd steal if necessary. We couldn't remember the day before, but we didn't care to live in the past. We lived for the present high with no concern for the future or memory of the past. We all used each other for money and rides and whatever the other one had that could get us closer to some weed. This meant we always owed someone. My sense of loyalty trapped me, and every day, the whole thing would start all over again: wake up, call friends, figure out how to find some weed.

I couldn't get out. Weed really did waste my life. Being stoned didn't make me happy; it made me numb. It released me from the trappings of my own head, from the fears of growing up.

Done with Mooches

One morning, I didn't call. I was sick of being called a loser and *being* a loser. Our addictions were stronger than our abilities to fulfill them. I'd even sold my Christmas presents to get weed, I was done with that cycle.

I started hanging out with this girl, Catherine, which helped, sort of, but it also drove me further in the wrong direction. She smoked me out and did acid, shrooms and DMT with me all the time (*DMT is a chemical that your brain releases when you sleep and causes you to dream. Smoking DMT in real life causes a dream-like effect in your vision and the way you think*).

The Back Story on Catherine

Catherine was a girl who Jax, Creed and I would call from time to time. She had a job, unlike us, and this meant she had money. Jax, Creed and I worked together to manipulate her into spending all her money on us. We fine-tuned our manipulation skills on her. She would spend thousands of dollars on drugs for us, and in return we gave her nothing. Maybe that's not how Creed or Jax saw the relationship but that is 100 percent how I looked at it, and I had no problem admitting it to myself. The end justifies the means. Before she hung out with me, she dated a homeless guy. Like me, he used her for what *he* wanted. He stole from her to sell stuff and keep the money; yet, she couldn't stop herself from calling him… until she met me.

After I started to only hang out with Catherine, I got a job. I convinced her to stop letting Creed and Jax mooch off of us— there was so much money all of a sudden. Catherine was kind. She just wanted to see others be happy. When we were high, we'd talk and laugh. We'd drive to nice destinations to smoke and take in the view of the Texas Hill Country. But drugs were all we did. I remember having good times, but I can't remember what those good times were.

She was my distraction, and I was hers. But, like always, I lost interest pretty quickly, and I moved on to other things that could distract me from the pain I was running from.

Pain

Not all the pain I was running from stemmed from Mary, the girl that had originally broke my heart. The pain came from a lot of things, some too small to write about. One juncture of pain in life caused me to run to other things which in turn would cause more pain. The pain in my life built upon itself over time and over little instances I had with friends and girls, all of which were completely hidden to my conscious mind thanks to different drugs and constantly smoking weed. Though this story quite often references me running from pain and worry, it's important to note that at the time, I didn't know I was running from anything; I thought I was only out having a good time. I never took the time to really analyze what was going on under the surface.

No Need for Reality

Sky returned from military school around that time and helped me avoid reality. Things were looking up for me. I had purchased a car by that point and was able to pick up Sky and drive us around to get whatever we needed to forget our life's worries. You guessed it, drugs. In addition to drugs, my old friend Jory bought us alcohol. Sky and I would drink and smoke every chance we got as well as do any other hard drugs we could find. Sky had gotten into using a needle and syringe to inject ecstasy into his veins, and I wanted to get him away from that. In the end, I ended up doing it myself.

Sky found a new place to live and stopped using needles to do drugs. We continued to take acid together and smoke weed for a time. Eventually, I got tired and annoyed of the crowd of people we typically hung out with. Sky and his friends were young and immature, I needed to find people that I thought I could hang out with and not feel like their babysitter.

I reverted back to Jory, who through this whole story supplied me with alcohol and was the first to sell me weed. I also started hanging out with a guy named T.

T was a cocaine user and seller, with whom I'd worked with at a Mexican restaurant before working at the restaurant with Jory. He'd give me gas money, and I'd drive him around in exchange for him getting me high on cocaine. Like me, T wanted to be young forever. He was 33, tall, black and had Bob Marley dreads. He sold weed and had blunts at the ready. He didn't like my friends, and they didn't like him—as per usual. So, I kept my friends separated.

Jory worked with me as a cook at a restaurant, small world. Jory had standards. He never got high or drunk before work. He listened with an open mind but voiced his opinion from time to time. He knew he was an addict, but he couldn't shake it. He was homeless and used to sleep in a tent in the woods when no one he knew would take him in. He'd wake up, go to work, get drunk, and go back to the woods. I drove him to get alcohol every day after work. Sometimes, we'd get cocaine, too. I knew it wasn't good for him to spend his money on drugs, but I didn't stop him. It was fun, and he would give me a portion of whatever he bought. We'd stay up and get high on whatever. He didn't smoke weed generally, but on many occasions I would try to get him to for some reason. "Naw, man. I don't do that," he would say, but that never stopped me from tricking him into smoking when he was really drunk or messed up on drugs.

Reverse Course

To admit what is wrong about yourself takes mental strength. It took you a long time to get where you are, so admitting it's all a waste is hard. Some people look back and think, W*hat happened?*

Where does the clean-up start? Anywhere.

When? Today.

My parents only saw me at night. They were disappointed in me, and they didn't know the half of it. They wanted their son back. They tried to make me love home by buying a pool table, soda, junk food and other things. They stopped trying to control me. They prayed for me, which disgusted me: "God, please let our son come home," ... *guh*. I hated it all.

I hated religion and Christians. They were just ignorant judges. One day when I was 14 or 15, just as I was getting into drugs, I smoked a cigarette on the steps of our church. I was testing the Christians, and most of them failed. Almost every person said a hateful word of what was to become of me. That's what I *heard* anyway. It pushed me further and further away from the church and religion in general.

Part III

God, Me and a Couple of Trips

When I was under the influence of many drugs, my mind would always wonder: *Why am I here in this world?*

First Line of Trippy Thought

Ideas flooded my mind while on drugs, and I got caught up in the analysis of the most minuscule details. I don't know if I became paranoid, but I did come up with some strange thoughts. I have included them here so the reader may better understand just how *out there* I really had become. Much of this has to do with the large number of psychedelics that I had been taking and used recreationally on weekends (*acid, shrooms, DMT, and others unnamed*).

When I would take hallucinogens, my mind drifted away from my once taught, "God is the creator." However, I always understood that something must come from something and so humanity must have come from some beginning. I reasoned out the ways aliens could be responsible for human creation/evolution:

> *If God doesn't exist,* I thought, *then the human race has only one sole purpose—to conquer the galaxy. Without religion, the human race collapses in on itself, which is why humanity needs to believe in "a god." If God doesn't exist but humanity does, then humanity came from the evolution of primates. Aliens probably saw the primal race becoming dominant on this planet, and jump-started evolution into the form of primate that we are today. Maybe that's why we have a missing link in the evolution chart. If humanity wasn't jump-started, we'd know we all came from primates, and there'd be no sense of right and wrong. Religion keeps beings in check and allows technological advancements which is why it would be in the interest of an alien race to jump-start our evolution.*

> *Now, the question remains: why would aliens want humans to prosper and populate? Why would they want humans to advance technologically?*

Three reasons.

1. *This planet is like farmland. Humans are the cattle. But then why would aliens let humans use so many resources? Why wouldn't aliens farm animals with more meat on them with less aptitude to fight back?*

2. *Earth is a military base, creating soldiers to fund the war effort of an alien race. Humans are basic—two arms and two legs. Humans have no claws, thus they must be the grunts on the front lines.*

But, if aliens could create soldiers why not create a fiercer one?
Every army needs its grunts, but if aliens could create heavy
infantry with no extra cost, why wouldn't they?
Also, why would aliens wait to reveal themselves to humans?
What does that accomplish?

3. *Humans would finally be accepted into intergalactic trade once*
   their brains advanced to the ability to fathom an other-worldly
   creature.
   But why would aliens want to trade if they could simply have
   taken over the planet?

Second Line of Trippy Thoughts
Relativity

Everything we see is true. Everything we see exists. But, everything we don't see is relative. In other words, nothing exists if it cannot be observed and thus proven. Sure, we know what's behind our heads, but you know it only theoretically. If someone silently destroyed it all, you'd still think it existed. Look at your surroundings, now close your eyes. As your eyes are close, how do you know that your surroundings are all the same from the last time your eyes were open? You don't. Now let's say as your eyes were closed, a silent nuke destroyed everything. But relative to you, whose eyes closed before the silent nuke, everything remains the same through the destruction.

Now what world exists? The one you remember, because reality belongs to the eyes of the beholder.

People define reality however they want, and most people decide to close their eyes at some point in life. Some people open them again, but most keep them shut.

Dimensions

We are our own dimensions. We think our thoughts are true. We think the color we call red is the way everyone else sees red, but is it? We give names to things, but we can't perceive the world through another person's eyes. We live in the universal dimension of time; yet, a long time to one is a short time to another.

Black Holes

Black holes are a mystery. I believed everything in the universe is a circle, so why not the universe itself? Imagine the universe as an expanding bubble that may or may never stop expanding. Black holes are stars that explode and suck in all matter—even light—with nothing escaping.

So, if the universe is a third-dimension bubble, then it can pop. When a star explodes, it creates a tear in our dimension that sucks everything in until it patches the tear. But where does all this matter go? To another dimension—one of only darkness. Then all that matter that plugged up the tear and closed the black hole continues to build until it yet again explodes, creating a new universe.

Think of the universe as soap—a bunch of bubbles (separate universes) stuck together. That's us.

Telepathy

I believed we could use our brains telepathically through belief. *If you want a pen to fly, think it completely. The trick is learning to think anything completely.*

If you anticipate losing a fight, you will. If you think you will fall, you will. If you think "I will not fall," you will catch yourself.

I believed acid allows the brain to think completely, that's why it was my favorite drug. If a tree talks to you, you think it's normal. If you talk to your friend inside his head by the way of your own thoughts, it's not freaky. Expectations and beliefs change, making anything possible.

God Who?

On drugs, I felt I could prove away God. Seeds of knowledge took over, and I couldn't control them.

One day I was watching TV and began to wander off in thought as I normally do. I was thinking that TV is almost completely *un*-entertaining for humans to watch. It easily loses all its pizzazz and becomes boring fairly quickly and often. If we were to evolve into a higher brain functioning human, there would be no way we would or could watch TV for entertainment. So, what would we do for entertainment?

Then it hit me. *What's more entertaining than watching the struggles of another? What's more entertaining than watching me, or humans in general? All my little faults and the way my brain works would be quite entertaining to another. Would they not?*

"It is pleasant," Lucretius once wrote, "when the sea is high; and the wind is dashing the waves about, to watch from shore the struggles of another."

Mankind has always had a fixation with the torment of other men. It was not that many years ago that mankind gathered together in the local town centers to watch public executions, such as the execution of Robert-François Damiens in 1757. This was a gruesome execution that hundreds of thousands of people gathered to witness as a form of entertainment less than 300 years ago.

A Word on Hallucinogens

Hallucinogens are weird and can lead to some pretty inexplicable things. Once, my friend and I communicated telepathically. We finished each other's sentences out loud. Anyone who normally takes hallucinogens will tell you this is a normal experience, yet no one will be able to explain to you how it's possible.

On acid (*a hallucinogen*), if you see a bush that needs water, you don't just see the exterior, you feel as if you travel inside the bush and analyze its interior needs. Your understanding of your situation is heightened, and you begin to look deeper into the meaning of all things around you. You go deeper into conversation, placement of things and people, lighting, volume—everything. These symptoms of the drug overwhelm people over the course of six or eight hours and can cause a bad trip. Someone describes a bad trip (*a "trip" is the allotted time that a hallucinogen affects the brain*) as if the drug takes over the mind, but someone describes a good trip as if the mind takes over the drug.

Every bad trip I've heard of includes the appearance of demons. Personally, I've never had what a bad trip, but I did encounter demons.

Trip 1

This section of the story marks one eventful night that would change my life forever. In December of 2011, I had decided to take acid with two friends of mine: Sky, whom I have written about, and Henry, who has not been mentioned up to this point. The events that unfolded on this night have become one of the lowest points of my drug career.

The location that we had decided on was Henry's home. His parents didn't care how loud we got or what we did in the house. As long as the cops didn't show up, his parents let us do whatever we wanted. At Henry's house, we each had three hits of strong liquid acid—enough for a 6-hour trip. Henry had no money for acid, so he was getting drunk through cheap liquor. Sky suggested we watch a crazy musical about love and so we put on the DVD and relaxed while letting the acid come over us. As the movie went on, I began to see a different message than the overall theme of love.

The musical told the story of a man caught between two worlds: the business world in which one gave up self-identity to pursue a job and became a cog in the system, and the world of his dreams and aspirations. The movie showed that either path he chose, none of it mattered because life is pointless, and the only thing you can do is find love.

The musical symbolized the dysfunction of the world, and in my own mind I had felt this same way about the world for a long time. *Either grow up and put on a suit or join the army and die like everyone else,* I thought. *Or, chase fame and money in a band. Either way, you're cornered.*

Henry didn't see that message—only Sky and I did. Henry experienced the meaning of the musical only on the surface, saying things like, "Yeah, it's good. I like this song."

Sky and I were miles deeper. The main character was me in every sense. I thought about that for a long time, then finally said it out loud. At the same time, Sky said, "Look, it's you, Keenan!" *Coincidence*, I thought, as I shrugged my shoulders and continued to watch.

From there, the movie portrayed the loop of the universe and how everything was connected from one part of life to the next. It felt so real, so true. I started to try and explain the concept to Sky and Henry. As soon as I finished, a character in the movie shouted, "You've got it!" This time, Henry freaked, and I realized that the movie speaking out on cue wasn't a coincidence… *If that wasn't a coincidence, then was Sky's comment about the character being me a coincidence?*

"I feel like *I'm* tripping," Henry said, drunkenly.

We laughed, but we were all unnerved. My thoughts seemed integrated with the movie. I would wonder if a certain thing were true, and characters would appear on screen at that moment and shout, "Yes!" I slowly started to come to the conclusion that all of what was going on was too perfectly timed to be a coincidence. I wanted to know what was going on. This seemed to be more than just a strange acid trip.

Just before the movie ended, a female character entered the screen and put her finger to her lips to say, "Shhhhhh." Just then, a door appeared on screen and opened. This beckoned me to discover more.

Sky yelled out, "Keenan, I can't go with you in there!" But, I continued to stare into the screen as the film traveled through the open door. This message was for me alone. The movie showed random stuff—roaches, ships, war, paintings, children laughing, screaming, dancers, all of which were each half-second clips. Meanwhile, my mind raced 1,000 thoughts per second with messages about my purpose in the world and the meaning of love.

Then, it ended.

I started laughing hysterically. It was overwhelming. Thoughts of perfection raced through my head—this perfect world, this perfect trip, this perfect mix of tripping and non-tripping individuals. At that moment, I looked around, and all was dark.

"What is this!? Where am I!?" I screamed.

Henry and Sky looked at each other strangely then looked back at me and said, "What are you talking about?" almost as if they knew something that I did not.

"Stop screwing with me. Tell me what this is!" I was screaming at the top of my lungs, then Sky got up, looked at Henry and said, "Okay," in a calm, soothing voice.

Henry warned Sky not to say a thing to me that I wasn't ready to know, but Sky ignored him and signaled for to me to follow him (without Henry noticing): *Come with me; I'll unplug you,* he mouthed without making a noise. I followed him out the door and into my car. Henry followed.

Sky said, "Wait. We need to get rid of him before we do anything." Then Henry joined us in the car. Sky put on a song.

"What are you doing? Let's go! Get me out of here!" I said.

Sky whispered, "Be quiet, or you aren't going anywhere."

Henry said, "Where are we going guys? Did he figure it out yet?"

Sky replied, "I don't know. We can't be direct. We're stuck, but we can talk now."

"Talk about what, are we all leaving?" I asked.

"If you can figure the way out of this neighborhood," Sky answered.

"What neighborhood?" I asked. I knew how to get out of Henry's neighborhood, since I had done it thousands of times, so Sky's words didn't make any sense.

"The stars are so pretty," Henry said. Then it clicked in my head—everything we hear and experience is no coincidence, not even Henry's comment on the stars. I deduced that we had to get out of this neighborhood of the *galaxy*.

"So how do we get out, Keenan?" Sky asked.

"How are we able to understand each other right now?" I asked.

"Because, we are here in the *car*," Sky said. In my mind, the *car* stood for *acid trip*.

"Well, then why do you guys need me?" I asked.

"You're the only one who can figure it out. Until then, we're all stuck here," Sky said. I thought he meant stuck inside our own brains or dimension.

"How can we talk to each other though?" I asked again.

"Because we can *see* each other," Sky said with a voice inflection, like I should know what he meant.

"How do we get out of this loop?" I asked.

"That's what we need *you* for," Sky said, laughing at the insanity.

"The only way would be a black hole, but that's impossible," I said.

"I know another way," Sky began, "but only if you're ready to get up and go."

Something whispered to me to expect a sign that would give me an instant to make up my mind. I heard a loud click, unlike any other, and I blurted out, "I want to go!"

A Quick Recap on the Craziness

1. I concluded that everything was happening for a reason. Nothing was a mere coincidence.
2. I believed the reality I was in was not a real reality and that it required escape.
3. Questioning reality made me vulnerable to false explanations.
4. I feared Sky and Henry both knew what reality was, but I was not allowed to know.
5. I thought Sky was going to show me what reality is.

"I don't want to go anywhere. Keenan, don't go," Henry said.

"Quiet" Sky said. "It's his choice." Sky took a CD out of my CD case.

"What are you doing?" I asked.

"Just wait," he said, as he flipped to a specific song on a CD that randomly showed up in my car a week earlier. I had no idea where it had come from. All the songs on it sounded the same, they were all weird instrumentals, so I didn't understand what he was searching for as he pressed "next" on my CD player until he came to a certain song.

Henry said, "I'm hungry I want a sandwich. I'm going inside." I realized the music was a subliminal message to get rid of Henry.

With Henry gone, Sky said, "Get up and go." He then threw open my car door and sprinted four houses down the block, and I followed him. He waited for me on the sidewalk. "You want to know what *this* is, Keenan?" he asked. When he said *this,* I understood it as reality.

"Yes," I said.

"This world is what you make it," he said and walked off. Questions flooded my mind.

I cried out in agony, "But what is the point?"

Sky stopped and turned to face me. "Let's go for a walk," he said.

We walked to a nature area where we had previously gone to smoke weed which was only 30 feet from us. Sky carried a flashlight as we passed under trees. I thought about how he had said he was going to "unplug" me.

I started to think about other dimensional creatures and the television. I began to take in the idea that I was just entertainment for somebody else's amusement. I had to test this thought and so I asked aloud, "Am I the only one?"

"No, there are many others like you," he replied. His response was confident, ambiguous, and it bit at my psyche.

"Can I have my flashlight back?" I asked.

"Why? Either it's on or it's off. Do you want it on, or do you want it off?" asked Sky. I took this as metaphorical, like: *Do you want further insight or not?*

"Keep it on," I said. We stopped in the middle of a dirt path. A break in the trees revealed an entire open field.

"So what is *this* exactly?" I asked.

"I already said I can't tell you. You have to figure it out for yourself," Sky replied.

"Okay. So, who am I?" I asked.

"I don't know, Keenan. Who *are* you?" Sky held the flashlight over my head shining down as he circled me.

"Am I a demi-god?" I asked, absolutely confused.

Sky laughed. "No, but *like* one." He sat down on the dirt. "Sit," he said. As he spoke, he put the flashlight up to the side of his face so I couldn't see his face but only the light which blinded me. "Hey, Keenan," a voice said, one I knew could only be Sky, yet it didn't sound like him anymore. "How ya doin' in there? I'm just checking in on you."

"God?" I asked, still completely confused at the situation.

"Close enough," he said, the flashlight shining in my eyes. He continued to talk, but his voice began to twist, "Are you being a good boy? Making sure to make the best of what you have in there even though it isn't much? I'm glad to see you. I'm glad that you finally are seeing truth. Be sure that you continue to take care of yourself in there." Suddenly, beyond the lit-up edges of Sky's face, I saw eyes peer from behind Sky's head. I started to ask what they were, but a loud screech interrupted me. It was indescribably ear piercing. I only saw the eyes for a millisecond, but they struck me with absolute horror. I was petrified. Unable to move. Unable to breathe. Frozen as if stuck within a picture frame. That moment has still never left me.

The eyes I saw were not human. They were jagged like knives and stared into me, absorbing all hope of escape. I felt like a rat in a cage. A rat that thinks itself invincible until it sees its master for the first time. The master then reaches in and squeezes the life out of the rodent just shy of the point of death, so the rat knows that nothing compares to its master's strength.

I felt naked, humiliated, pathetic, weak, insignificant, hopeless of escape, all within a single glance of those eyes. Sky looked at my mouth gaping in horror and laughed hysterically.

"I'm sorry," he said. "I had to do it just once." I was confused. "C'mon, let's go to the football bleachers."

"I'm not going anywhere with you," I said.

"As if that matters," Sky rattled back.

"What are you talking about?" I asked.

"Keenan, you still haven't figured it out?" he said, still in a voice that was not his own. "You're the smartest person here. You're the *only* one here. Nothing is real, and nothing exists." I remembered back to the thought I had days before—about the other beings being amused by human struggle. "You're a joke. You're a dog chasing his tail. This is all you," Sky said, opening his arms up like he was holding the world. "I'm just your consciousness."

"So, you're not here?" I asked.

"I'm here as much as you want me to be, Keenan. Everything is all relative. Have you ever seen the back of your head?" he chuckled as though he had just pricked the end of an inside joke.

"No," I answered.

"You're plugged into a machine to see how long it takes you to figure it out. You're the funniest thing around. Everyone is always trying to tell you you're in a box, yet you never understand. It's hilarious!" Sky said. "Didn't you hear the people banging on the walls while we were watching the movie? Beyond what you can see is where they hide." I remembered that there had been loud, inexplicable bangs coming from the walls during the movie. "Now come on. Let's go to the bleachers."

I realized everything was relative to our location—the sounds, the sights... everything (again, no coincidences). We stood at a path that opened to a field. The area behind represented home. The path represented my choice. And, the field represented a new reality.

"Look, Keenan. I can run this way or that way. All you're doing is staying put." While saying this, he ran freely in the field and ended his run, inches from my face.

"Then how do I get out of here?" I asked.

"Simple," he replied. "Kill yourself now that you've figured it out. Then, you become reborn and begin again. You're feeling that déjà vu? All that is, is just residual memories from your previous lives. Come! It's time to leave," Sky said in the midst of me feeling the strongest déjà vu I had ever felt in my life. I knew this meant it was time to kill myself.

"Wait!" I cried out from the path, "I don't normally have time like this. I need to use it to figure this out. I need to find a way out of this cage."

"I told you. There's only one way out. Now, come. Let's take your last walk in this world," he said.

"What if I don't kill myself?" I asked.

That question prompted a rant of countless things spoken out loud by Sky, all of which I knew he was going to say before he spoke them. Each thing he listed would remind me of my captivity in the cage and my ability to think of his words before their utterance sealed my belief. "Birds chirp during the day and crickets in the night, because without them, you'll hear us," he said. "This world is a cage for your mind. You want change, but do you see how your friends do not?" he asked.

I thought back to my childhood. It was so perfect, and my parents loved me so much.

"Your parents are just programmed to love you," Sky responded to my thoughts. "Haven't you ever wondered why your childhood was perfect? Because love is what you seek and all you can do. It's the only thing that makes this place bearable for you. It's the only real thing." He continually spoke my thoughts exactly as I thought them.

I felt suicide was my only option. Then, a thought entered my head.

"Go back!" it said. "This is nothing but a drug. In the morning, the sun will rise again." Without speaking, I turned and walked away.

Sky screeched and screamed after me, but I ignored the inhuman sounds and continued walking. I lost strength with each step. Every step made me feel 50 pounds heavier. Gradually, I could see the street from where I came from. Behind me, I heard Sky's voice say, "You'll never forget! Drugs won't help you forget! *We* will always be there!"

I reached the tree line. One more step would bring my whole world down and put me back in the theatre of my tormentors. I summoned all of my physical and mental strength to leave the "truth" behind me and embrace the "ignorant lie" before me. I felt stuck. Then, I heard a voice: "I am the Truth, and there is no other." With that, I knew what to do. "I'm going back," I said, my chest feeling restricted as if by weights. My voice came out twisted and low.

"Keenan, wait!" Sky screamed before falling to the ground. I looked and saw the creature with the devilish eyes leap through Sky and off into the darkness. That instantaneous sight of the creature caused me to run away full-speed. "Keenan!" I heard Sky cry, as if he were being boiled alive. I ran halfway back to my car parked in front of Henry's home. Sky came sprinting at me. I stared in fear. Fight or flight kicked in, and I ran at him head-on. We both stopped at the last second before impact, meeting each other eye to eye, inches from each other.

"You can't run, Keenan. Why would you run from the truth? It's what you asked for," Sky's voice had finally returned to his own.

"I can't believe it. I won't believe it," I said.

"Why?" he asked.

I thought, *Because if that's true, then everyone's as insane as I am,* but I didn't say it.

"If it's true, that means I'm just as insane as you? Is that why Keenan?" he asked with a grin as though he knew he had read my mind.

These mind games had gone on long enough. A car sped around the corner.

"C'mon. Let's go back," Sky said.

It's just acid, I said to myself as I followed a few paces behind.

I started to think about the movie we watched, I saw the loop of the universe within my thoughts through the memory of the movie, the loop I was stuck in. The movie spoke of how love is all life is worth, of friends being there for you when you are hurt, of not locking yourself in a closet just because nothing worked out the way you planned it. The movie spoke of how there are fields of people just like me stuck in a box for a joke, so though you are alone you are not the only one. And no matter how bad you feel, a good shot of love will dose you right back to normality. This is the loop of the universe. This is the loop and inescapable reality of my insanity. The past is there to control the future, to prepare me for the future. Everything that happened in the past happened for a reason though I may not know the reason at the moment. Everything is planned out. There is not a single thing my eyes have seen that they were not meant to see, for I have seen these things so I may be aware. But if I am truly the only one, *aware of what?* I thought to myself, *There must be something bigger going on than what Sky just spoke to me.*

Back at Henry's

We returned at 3 AM to find Henry awake on the couch watching TV. We sat beside him. Three loud thuds came from the wall that shared a side with the outside of the house. Whatever banged on that wall was more powerful than a human knock. Henry looked at me.

"What was that, Keenan?" Henry asked as though talking to a child. Sky smirked.

"The neighbors," I said. They laughed, as if they knew I was denying reality, and I was. I was done with their so-called "truth." I went back to playing stupid, watching commercials—every one of them about people who did the wrong thing and tried to get back on track with their lives. *Are these directed at me?* I wondered.

"You need to get help. There's someone you can call," the commercials said.

"Going back to your parents would be hilarious," Sky said in response to my thoughts on who I could call. "No one will believe you."

Coming Down

The trip was over after six hours, and I had school in the morning, so I drove home. With every blink, the creature appeared beneath my eyelids, burned into my sight, like when you stare at a light but continually see the outline of the bulb after looking away. It was horrible. At home, sleep was impossible. The creature kept reappearing and haunted me. I stayed up until dawn and got ready for school. *Who cares?* I thought. *None of it's real.*

The Next Day

I was twenty minutes late for school, but I had to talk to someone for some sort of confirmation. I saw Mark walking alone toward his classroom. We hadn't spoken for at least a year, but I had to talk to someone. I was convinced that seeing him in the hallway twenty minutes late was no coincidence.

"What's up man," he said.

"I need to talk to you." I answered.

"Dude, I'm busy," he said, rattling off excuses.

"Too bad," I said. "I'm coming over after school." We bumped fists and walked our different ways.

The creature still strobed through my vision. In class, I traced it from the image burned into my retina.

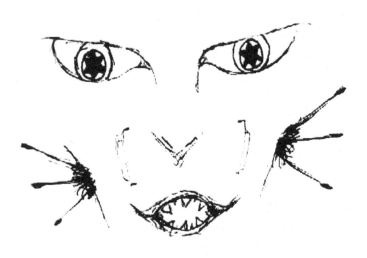

This is that tracing

Although I was very sure that my mentality had been corrupted by the acid, I still wondered what was real and what wasn't. After school, I told Mark everything—about how nothing is real, and I didn't know what to do. He didn't contradict me, and that scared me even more.

We went to go skate with my old friends, Ben, Creed, Matt, David, Jax, and some others. I commented something like, "I never wanted to do drugs again."

They all laughed and said, "Whatever, Keenan. You *love* drugs." I couldn't deny it.

I was so distressed from everything that was going on, unable to find comfort for my mind. For four days, I stayed home when I wasn't at school. Although I lived with my parents, my parents hadn't seen me home that long in years. In school, everyone acted sympathetic toward me for some reason. Their gaze softened, and they all seemed lost. I felt their emotions and constantly caught them looking at me. I wondered, *If I'm the one in the box, and these people are my imaginings, of course they would want to gawk at me.*

I remembered from my trip that love was the only thing that could make this life bearable. Before, I had thought love meant sex, so I stopped having sex to spite the system. But, truly, I had never loved a person more than I loved weed. I was incapable of it. I didn't want to get attached to anybody like I had gotten attached to Mary. Girls and friends were useful; anything more was a burden.

Back to It

I started in on drugs again as the weeks went on (minus the acid). The trauma from the trip slowly healed to a faint memory. I decided to forget to remember that I was lying to myself. I started having sex again with the girl I was with at that time. It was only as I started to be with her again that I began to forget what Sky had said to me that night. At first, I thought *I've proven what he said about love is real, that it's the only way to forget the box I was trapped in,* but slowly my thoughts turned to, *What did Sky tell me again when I was on acid?*

I truly had forgotten everything. My brain denied and locked up that night deep within my subconscious. The only thing I could remember was that I had forgotten something important. I couldn't bear the sight of Sky, so we drifted apart. I hung out with Jory, David (Ben's brother), T (occasionally, when he needed help selling) and Trevor (sometimes). I picked up right where I'd left off, driving Jory around for booze, staying up all night, getting drunk and high, then going to work. The life I was living was pathetic, I was only making enough money to live paycheck to paycheck.

One day I was with David at his place, and he had a bag full of some shake weed (*the last bit of weed, like crumbs*). He was having trouble selling it, so he asked me to sell it for him because he knew that I could. The bag contained two ounces of weed, which was a lot, but I needed the money. So, I agreed to do it.

I hadn't sold weed for almost three years, but it didn't take long to find customers. I sold the whole load in a week.

The next time I got more weed, I got it from a different dealer. I moved four ounces in four days. I was back at the same rate I used to be, making good money. I bought a scale for measuring out weed, a couple of containers for holding product, and I bought a few pipes. I was back in the drug dealing game and this time it felt like I was doing it all for me.

Selling drugs erased the last of the acid trip from my memory. Within six months, drugs and sex were right where they'd always been.

Graduating High School

Somewhere in the haze of weed and cocaine, I graduated. As you could probably guess, I was the only one out of all my friends to do so. I wanted so badly to walk across that stage and prove I wasn't a burnout, but that didn't happen. I didn't walk, because a teacher failed me on account of my unacceptable reports on the legalization of weed, implementation of communist dictatorship in public schools and the non-existence of God. I had to take summer school, which I did. In the end, I did graduate high school, I had nothing to show for it— no walk across that stage, no ambition, no future.

Trip 2

My tripping days were not over. Soon enough, I made another bad decision in my life. Yep, you guessed it—I took more acid. During this time, I had been selling high amounts of weed to a few loyal customers. Some of these costumers allowed me and other friends to join in smoking the weed I sold to them. That's where this next story takes place—in a customer's home whom I had taken a liking to. This final acid trip leads me to the very bottom of that pit I had been digging for so many years, and it's where I would eventually come face to face with so many things that I had been running from.

I was with Jory and a kid named Tack at a house owned by two other people who were my customers. Tack was an old friend of Jory's I'd had since I knew Mark, and these customers were their friends. At some point, a conversation about acid arose, and it turned out everyone knew the same acid dealer. We all decided to go over there and buy some acid for the night, though I was hesitant.

I bought three hits. Tack bought one. Jory bought one, the other guy bought four, and his girlfriend decided not to trip. I had decided to trip because the guys we were with said he'd buy me two hits. Before we took the acid, I said to everyone, "I don't remember what happened last time I was on acid, but I don't want to be alone with anyone. I need to know that y'all aren't going to mess with me."

They said they wouldn't. We took the acid, but none of us seemed to be tripping even after waiting for hours. The owner of the house who had taken four hits, wasn't tripping either, so he and his girlfriend went to his room and passed out. He said we could stay there at his house, but Jory didn't want to stay. He drove home.

So, there I was, at a stranger's house on three hits of acid that wasn't making me—or anyone—hallucinate. It was just me and Tack left by ourselves. We went outside to smoke a cigarette, and a thought came into my mind: *Everything looks so fake and plastic. Is this all real?* I closed my eyes and thought, *Okay, Keenan. If this is fake, I should be able to fly if I believe I can.* I opened my eyes and was still on the ground. Reality check passed.

Then Tack said, "Everything looks fake, doesn't it? It all looks plastic." He kept repeating that until I agreed with him. *Strange,* I thought, *was that a coincidence?*

Back in the house, MTV was on. Tack cleaned the living room, and I began to put weed into a bong so we could continue smoking. He finished cleaning, sat down and said, "Look, Keenan. Everything is clean. Now we can get down to some good weed smoke." I laughed at his phrasing.

On MTV, five music videos played with no commercial interruptions—bizarre. The first four were crazy with red flashing lights and huge crowds. Every song talked about how great it was to be on stage. "It's a party. Come join us." They talked about, "More, more, more." More sex, more good times and the pointlessness of life without these things.

The fifth video had blue and green hues, the colors alone were comforting. It wasn't a crowd but a band in a room that sang of God and His greatness, same channel. Tack stood up and put his hands over his ears as if the song were hurting him.

"I don't like this song," Tack said. "I can't stand it. It sucks!"

"Well, I thought it was comforting," I replied.

He turned off the TV. "Are you kidding? Don't you hate that song?" He stood there in silence and stared at me. He walked around a table to another couch. The owners of the house had a little Chihuahua, who had hopped in a seat directly across from me, chased its tail in a circle, then sat down, looked at me and smiled.

In that instant, I remembered everything Sky had said—that I'm just a dog chasing my own tail. This was the reminder Sky had told me would happen. Inside, I freaked out, but externally, I stayed calm. Déjà vu hit me hard, as if I had been in this exact scenario before. As if I had lived through this already.

Tack's head twitched toward my direction as if a switch and been flipped. His head tilted ten degrees to the left as the edges of his mouth raised ever so slightly. He sat there, staring into my eyes, half smirking as though he knew what I did not.

He asked, "What are you gonna do?"

"Peace, man," I said. "I'm going home."

Tack was awestruck. "You know what I'm talking about, Keenan. Are you sure?" Something about his voice had changed, yet I felt as though I heard it before.

I opened the door and closed it behind me as Tack yelled my name, "Keenan!" in the same voice I had heard come from Sky in the woods.

I continued to my car, and the second I sat down in it, I felt as though I started tripping hard. Acid doesn't usually last more than six hours, and it had already been that long. Everything began to spin. The world seemed to collapse in all of its dimensions. Things became wide then narrow. My eyesight was shot, but I drove. Then, I looked up at the sky and saw what appeared to be a slit in the clouds in the shape of a half opened eye, like the one on the top of the pyramid on the back of the one dollar bill. In the center was a cloud that had been lit up by the rising sun in the shape of the circle resembling an eyeball. The shadows moved on the clouds in such a way that I felt as though I was being looked down upon by some huge sentient being's eye. I felt very small and insignificant. It was the same feeling I had when looking into the eyes of the creature on the first acid trip.

The eye looked down at me. I couldn't think straight, I was filled with panic.

I turned up the radio, looking for some kind of distraction, but I still felt like a hamster in a hamster wheel, running in place. I changed the radio by decimal frequencies until I'd completed the two-mile drive home. As I pulled up to my house, I wanted to yell for help. I heard a voice once more, this voice also sounded familiar. It was the voice that beckoned me to turn around and walk back when I was on the dirt path in the woods with Sky. "I am the rock of salvation, I will not move. When all other things are shaken and fall, I alone remain."

In the back of my head, I knew whose voice this was, and I knew this voice was God. I replied to the voice, "God, if you're real, show up, because if you don't, I'm going to kill myself. But if you're real, I'll give you everything I have."

I was just as sure to kill myself as I was to give all to God— not like I felt like I had anything of note to give.

Suddenly, I didn't feel safe. I felt like the creatures could hear me, the one that spoke through Sky and the one I was certain of spoke through Tack. I kept my head down and continued to talk to that voice, to talk to God. As I did, my tongue spoke a language I couldn't understand. I could sense my speech forming sentences that had flow and rhythm. (I learned later that this happened in the New Testament in the book of Acts.)

God Undeniable

What happened in the car? I had run into a T-intersection on the road of life, with the ability to turn left or to turn right; the road would no longer continue to go straight. I could no longer continue living my life the way I had been. When I cried out to God in abandonment, leaving behind my old life, something happened. I can't explain it, I felt it. As if a bolt of lightning had struck me. I knew in that moment that God was real. Somehow it was confirmed within the deepest parts of me. My soul? I don't know. But what I do know is that in that moment in my car, He made Himself undeniably known.

As I continued to talk, the radio seemed to play louder, but it wasn't playing a song. Two people came across the radio and spoke.

"What is he doing now?" one voice said.

"Sounds like he's crying," the other answered.

"He sounds like a baby. He can't even talk right," the first one said.

"Awwe, poor baby. Life isn't what you wanted, and now you're crying," the other said.

"Go cry to your mom, little boy," the first one said. I stopped speaking completely and was horrified.

"That's better," I heard. "Now at least he stopped.

I turned the radio off. I was angry and expected it might turn back on. I wanted to pray/talk to God again, but I was scared something else would attack. I looked down, and my hand had a huge cut on it. Suddenly, I remembered Sky saying, "Would you rather be rid of this place or deal with your cuts and bruises? Why live with scars when you can just restart?"

I walked toward the door and said, "I'd rather live with the cut. I'd rather live with the scars."

I saw my cat as I entered the house. "Hi, Max. Don't let anyone else in here," I said.

My mom was lying down on the couch. "Hi, Keenan," she said. I didn't reply and just headed toward my room. A warm breath ran up my neck, and I heard the exhale of a person. It sent shivers down my spine and cast the warmth into every atom of my body. That sensation still sticks with me today. It didn't scare me, it comforted me. Actually, it gave me peace—peace that allowed me to ignore what wasn't real. I felt relaxed, calm and serene, which was weird.

I opened my bedroom door, turned on the lights, and my brother Garrett shot up from under the covers. It didn't look like him; his skin looked fake, pixelated like an old video game. In fear, I turned the lights off and ran to my bed. Now, in addition to Garrett and me in the room, creatures slithered and crept all over. I couldn't make them out in the darkness, but I saw glimpses of light reflecting off their backs from the moonlit window. I didn't want to move.

"Garrett, can you turn on the light?" I asked.

"What?" he answered, groggily. There was no way he was going to do it.

Just get out of here. I'm not sleeping here, I thought. I grabbed pillows and blankets and bolted toward the door. The only light in the house was a dimly lit ceiling light hovering over my mom, who was sleeping on the couch. I lay next to her on the adjacent couch.

"Where have you been?" she asked.

When she asked me where I had been, I immediately wanted to say everything that had happened and was happening to me, but another thought came to my mind. I remembered what Sky had said, that if I go to my parents, *they* would think that everything that had happened was funny--silly, even. I decided to defy the demonic creature voices even though it felt like that was admitting they were right. I thought a step of defiance would be a step closer to the breath of peace I felt on my way in the house. I told my mom I was on acid, and that I didn't want to do drugs anymore. I was tired of lying and not speaking to my family. My burden was heavy and had made me mad at the world long enough. My mom had physically given me life, I think that's why I chose to confess to her—she was a representation of God to me.

Salvation

This book is not about demons, drugs, or even bad choices in life. This book is all about this moment: salvation. In this moment of confession, I laid everything I was and had been, down on the ground. I came humbly, acknowledging that all my life up to this point had been for naught. I willfully admitted my inability to control my own life with any sort of meaning. Though the confession was in front of my mom, I was confessing to God. The empire I had built that I called my life, my achievements, my desires, my goals, my image, I tore down before God and told Him that He now had the right to build where I once had. My life was to be part of His Kingdom, and it started here, destroying the structures I had erected myself. Salvation starts here, at confession.

Throughout my confession, my mom stayed calm and quiet. I couldn't express how sorry I was. At the end, she closed her eyes and tried to go back to sleep, but I kept calling her name— just to know I wasn't alone. She wouldn't answer, but when I would peer over my pillow at her, she'd open her eyes and look at me. Voices told me that this was only because my gaze put her into existence. I tried to sleep, but I couldn't. My brain was running like mad. I got up and drew the picture below.

I didn't know what I was drawing, but I couldn't shake this image from my mind. I felt like I had been maimed but rescued. I realized I had drawn a self-portrait of my current state.

As I drew, a memory rushed back to me—the time when I told God, "I'm leaving you. The devil will show me a demon before You show me Your face." A horrid feeling came over me. *Did I see a demon?*

I lay back down on the couch and stared into the darkness of my eyelids and called the name of Jesus.

At one point, I thought I was asleep, and I dreamed that the Lord and the devil were speaking to each other. The Lord boasted about my strength, but the devil claimed that all the wrong things I'd done were okay in moderation. The Lord talked of a beautiful life with Him and how all things are possible. But, the devil butted in, extolling the value of spice in life. God described how spice misplaced ruins the flavor of everything.

I opened my eyes to see the morning news on TV. Two cooks were on the screen—one in black holding some spices over a dish and the other in white. "Back to you," one of them said, directing the broadcast back to the anchors.

"And now some clips from our favorite movies," one of the anchors said. The scene was of the Terminator saying, "I'll be back." Another clip showed a hand withering away to the wind. No coincidences; I took this as a message from God about the devil. One of the reporters said, "Well, he's not back right now."

"Yep," the other anchor said, "and we're pretty much all safe and sound under his roof." *They're talking about God!* I thought.

Just then, my dad walked down from a dimly lit hallway with an angry look on his face. I assumed he heard what I had told my mother. He didn't say anything as he proceeded to the kitchen for coffee and food. He returned down the hallway back to his room.

I heard loud thuds repeatedly coming from my parents' room. Not one or two, but several. A voice in my head said, "Fear not. Your father is not in trouble. He's doing what a father does best, defending you against demons." The voice again felt familiar. The voice sounded as though I had heard it before, like a calling from afar. The voice sounded like the warm peaceful breath I had felt on my neck. The voice wasn't just heard with my ears but with my entire body, my entire soul as though everything I was could somehow partake in this voice.

"God?" I said in disbelief.

The message back was something like, *Yes. Your oppressors are destroyed for now. I am with you as you rest in my truth and light. Now rest.*

I didn't know what to think. I still felt like the only one alive—the only one who existed. I felt like the devil was trying to get me to kill myself through lies mixed with truth, but I didn't know what was true. I felt abandoned yet loved. The voice in my head repeated, "I am with you. You are never alone."

Part IV
War and Peace

Reconciliation

For the next three days, I was so tired and sore that I couldn't move. All I could do was lie down and think.

I was assured I was safe, but I still struggled to sleep, worrying about what lurked in the darkness and feeling ill-equipped to fight this evil that felt too close for comfort. Then, I heard a voice tell me there was a weapon that has been with humanity for centuries: The Bible. I found a Bible in my parent's study and didn't know where to begin. I randomly opened it to Psalm 91.

> *Surely he will save you from the fowler's snare and from the deadly pestilence. He will cover you with his feathers, and under his wings you will find refuge; his faithfulness will be your shield and rampart. You will no longer fear the terror of the night, nor the arrow that flies by day, nor the pestilence that stalks in the darkness, nor the plague that destroys at midday.*
>
> Psalms 91:3 -6

I slept with the Bible on my chest every night. When it fell, I woke up and repositioned it. I couldn't put it down. I read the

New Testament Gospels about Jesus' ministry. It seemed everything I read was directed toward me. I realize now, it's to all humanity.

For those three days, I lay there and read. I was living this verse:

> *Come to me, all you that are weary and are carrying heavy burdens, and I will give you rest. Take my yoke upon you, and learn from me; for I am gentle and humble in heart, and you will find rest for your souls. For my yoke is easy, and my burden is light.*

Matthew 11:28-30

As I rested, people called me to come get high or do drugs—people I hadn't talked to in years. The devil was trying to suck me back in any way possible. Everyone had excuses why I needed to go hang out with them.

There were at least four so-called crazy parties going on, but for once in my life I was content with what I had. I had sat behind that wheel of the red-hot Camaro, I had drifted backwards down that hill and I was never going to sit behind that wheel again, not by myself anyway.

The calls and texts became a nuisance. I changed my number and deleted my drug contacts. The temptation was gone at the moment, but I remembered the TV saying, "I'll be back," which I took as a warning.

My parents were concerned, learning that I'd sold weed. I gave everything to my dad to throw away even though it was worth some coin. God assured me that there would be better things to come, and I had complete faith in that. God wasted no time, showing me the better things.

These next few sections in this chapter are some of those better things that the Lord taught me in those three days as I prayed, rested and listened. I want to share these better things with you, the reader and I beckon you to seek these same things from the same God. This section is filled with truths and petitions. Do not read this section to simply get through this book. Take your time and commit yourself to dwelling on what is presented.

Good and Evil

It's easy to live by what one judges to be right rather than what *God* says is right. Sin can be confused with truth when man makes truth in his own image. Truth is God, not man.

Man's truth is confusing—to the point of justifying infanticide. We have the opportunity to listen to God's truth. There's a battle raging between truth and deception. God invites you into His eternal life, and the devil tells you humanity isn't worth it. Every choice pushes you closer to or further from God. There is no decision that stands on neutral ground. Who determines good and evil? God.

> *For since the creation of the world, God's invisible qualities-his eternal power and divine nature-have been clearly seen, being understood from what has been made, so that people are without excuse… The requirements of the law are written on their hearts, their consciences also bearing witness, and their thoughts sometimes accusing them.*
>
> Romans 1:20, 2:15

You can deceive yourself, but not God. God is truth and the foundation of the existence of what we think of as right and wrong. The fact that good and evil even exist is proof enough that God exists. Why wouldn't you kill a person who disagrees with you? Because we are not descendants of primates dictated by evolutionary desires. No, we are the descendants of God himself for He is called our Father, and His Son, our brother (Matthew 12:50). It is not the laws of man written on the hearts of men, it is the laws of God that are written on the hearts of men.

Spiritual Warfare

How did I get to this point where I don't care about right and wrong? I wondered. *Since when did I desire to do cocaine?* I didn't grow up wanting to do it; it was a progression.

When I felt abandoned by Mary, the one girl I thought I loved, I pulled away from everyone I loved. This led to falsehoods and destructive habits. I friend-hopped for better access to weed, and my habit grew. Then, pride pushed me into doing drugs through my nose and up my veins.

The devil works progressively. Girls didn't use to dress like sluts. People didn't curse in common discourse. Getting high was once considered wrong. Pre-marital sex was unacceptable. Now, music promotes prostitution and every kind of evil. No need to be sly—no one cares.

It's sad. Now, God is the one sneaking back into culture because men have turned their backs on God and have begun to look at one another for self-approval. Even the worst sinners can find someone to surround themselves with that are, if not as bad, worse off than they are. Hiding in plain sight, unashamed of their own sin.

When man sins, if he is not going to repent, he will quickly look for other men that sin, in order to appease his conscience.

Look, what I'm doing isn't bad, all these other people think the same way as I do. This form of thinking leads man down a road without any objective morality and is the reason we can look at society and see groups of individuals committing the most heinous of sins. It's not that they don't believe in God; they're ignoring Him.

Some of them may even admit that they believe in God. I told myself I believed in God even while I was snorting cocaine. Salvation doesn't come to those who say they believe, but rather those who follow. It doesn't matter if you *know about* Jesus, the question is; do you *know and follow* Jesus?

> *For although they knew God, they neither glorified him as God nor gave thanks to him, but their thinking became futile and their foolish hearts were darkened. Although they claimed to be wise, they became fools… Furthermore, just as they did not think it worthwhile to retain the knowledge of God, so God gave them over to a depraved mind, so that they do what ought not to be done. They have become filled with every kind of wickedness, evil, greed and depravity. They are full of envy, murder, strife, deceit and malice. They are gossips, slanderers, God-haters, insolent, arrogant and boastful; they invent ways of doing evil; they disobey their parents; they have no understanding, no fidelity, no love, no mercy. Although they know God's righteous decree that those who do such things deserve death, they not only continue to do these very things but also approve of those who practice them.*
>
> Romans 1:21, 28-32

Somehow, people justify their behavior in light of God's unconditional love. Yes, God loves unconditionally, but He's also a just judge. The devil is the prince of lies who draws you to him in the lake of fire.

Devil Prints

I encourage the reader at this time, go back to PART II and read it in light of there being an entity that was always trying to pull me deeper into sin. During PART II, there are not many mentions of God's unfailing ability to give me ways out because I wasn't looking for them, but I can assure you now they were always there. But the devil was just as prevalent. Constantly, he was there luring me down paths I had no intention of going down.

Drugs, timely friendships, hate for my mom ... it all came from outside influences and forces. Those intentions weren't inborn in me. My parents introduced me to God. To be separated from God, I needed to be separated from the people who brought me to Him: my parents. Clearly, I'm not the only one who revels in war-game strategies. Otherwise, there wouldn't have been people and opportunities perfectly timed in my life to take me to the next level of hell. We always need to be on guard in our lives. Be aware of our own decision-making power and the impact it has on our trajectory. The devil is as real as God. In this life, you can't have one without the other, and both are constantly fighting over you.

God desires you would find pleasure in him. He finds pleasure in you.

God is in every breath, every blink and every step you take. Everything you see in this world exists under God's sovereignty. Nothing on this earth is inherently evil. He said in Genesis that all He created was good. But, man takes that which is meant for good and does evil.

> *For our struggle is not against flesh and blood, but against the rulers, against the authorities, against the powers of this dark world and against the spiritual forces of evil in the heavenly realms.*

Ephesians 6:12

To follow Christ is to become a vessel of God to do His will. If you are with God, He will speak through you to the world to help light the way. The same goes for the devil. If you're going through your life in sin without repentance, you're one of the devil's tools, able to speak on his behalf. If you're high, drunk or living in sin, the devil gains a foothold over you.

I believe the devil used me to do many things for him without my knowing. When I was constantly smoking weed around Jory, for some reason I always had the desire to try and get him high as well. The devil is always looking for ways to attack, and he will use the people that he already owns to coax others in.

One thing for certain is that God never leaves us alone. I can look back and see how God provided a way out at each point of decision, and, just the same, the Devil provided paths that lead further down the trail of destruction. The sad part is I never took the road less traveled, but one thing was for certain: the choice of who I followed and who I let into my heart was always mine to make.

What Following God Looks Like

I didn't consider weed a drug. That's the story of humanity: we call evil good. If there is a deceiver in the world known as the devil, his goal would be to make humanity lose their ability to differentiate between good and evil.

People say, "I believe in God," and use that as an insurance policy against a fiery death. But, God is holy, and we are called to be holy (set apart) as He is holy. If we believed, we'd pray constantly. We'd never stop seeking His face. We'd dress modestly and control our mouths. We wouldn't stomp on God's grace by continuing to sin without regard. No, we'd say, "Lord, save me. I want to do Your will."

A true believer in Christ may sin but he does not go on sinning. Conviction grips him, takes hold of every action of his life and drives him toward the cross. Repentance, turning from sin, is his desire. Eyes that have seen Christ seek no other thing but Christ, because no other thing can satisfy. If your eyes have seen the goodness of God, then they have reached their fullest potential; nothing comes close to fulfilling them again. To be with God is the only thing worth doing once a man has experienced Him—and I thought drugs were addicting.

I'm still an addict, and I have found the one substance that I can't get enough of in my system: Jesus—and He never runs dry. I'm writing this five years after this experience, and, still to this day, Jesus satisfies all my desires.

Our God is ineffable (words can't describe) and ineffably beautiful—inexplicable—like a color a person has never seen before. He has a plan to redeem creation and wants you to be a part of that. He places a desire in a person's heart to seek Him, but it's up to each person to respond.

Following God put a new desire in my heart to be used as in instrument. As I prayed, new words came from my mouth, words I had never thought before: "Crucify me, Lord. I am your humble servant here to do Your good in this world." I no longer desired sinful things like I once did. I desired to do what God desired of me.

Seven Deadly Sins

It also dawned on me that I was living all seven deadly sins taught by the Church.

1. WRATH

I lived in wrath every day. I hated life and didn't care if I died. All was pointless. And my only job was to cope with life. Malice and wrath filled my worldview and fueled my fire.

2. GREED

Greed consumed my mind. I didn't care about anyone or anything outside of my next drug. And, I wanted it all to myself. Other people were merely more mouths to feed, more people I had to share my drugs with.

3. SLOTH

My friends and I were straight-up lazy. Once, I was smoking with a group too lazy to put more weed into the pipe, so we stopped. We didn't have real jobs. We just smoked and zoned out. If we did something, it wasn't productive or skill-building. Going places became a hassle unless it's for the purpose of getting more drugs. If I couldn't buy fast food, eating wasn't worth it.

4. PRIDE

Pride is the easiest to fall into and the most detrimental of all seven (in my opinion), especially for a drug addict. It's so easy to place yourself above others. Drug dealers sometimes think their customers worship them, because they're the big, bad dealer. People who do hard drugs look down on people who just smoke weed. Weed smokers rank themselves against each other based on commitment and tolerance. It's all pride.

5. & 6. LUST & GLUTTONY

Lust and gluttony go hand in hand. Both are never satisfied in a constant battle for more, more, more. Lust emerges from a false attempt to fill a hole in the heart. People fill it with sex and drugs, but that rips the hole even wider to accommodate all the new loneliness and sadness those things bring in. Then, a person has to cover all those new feelings with more false satisfaction: "Let's go to the bar," "Let's smoke some weed and relax." The only thing that can fill that hole is God—and trust me, I never thought I'd be saying that.

People who live unto themselves are dead—even though their flesh thrives with resources. All of their pleasurable things do not satisfy the soul.

One person dies in full vigor, completely secure and at ease, well nourished in body, bones rich with marrow. Another dies in bitterness of soul, <u>never having enjoyed anything good</u>.

Job 21: 23-25

My Changed Mind

Anytime one of my friends "found Jesus," it was so confounding. I'd hear, "Yeah, that kid got saved; he's not the same," and ask *What? How is that even possible? Found Jesus? What does that mean? You need some God just to be able to live your life—that's just sad.* But, it's true. We need God to fill that void in our lives. We try to stuff so many things to fill the void, but no one ever wants to try God—the only thing that can fill it.

We were built to be in relationship with Him. It allows us to trust someone besides ourselves who is actually worthy of trust. Every time, He rises to the occasion. Just ask God to prove His existence to you. He is ALWAYS looking for an opportunity to show you who He is.

I love them that love me; and those that seek me early shall find me.

Proverbs 8:17 (KJV)

7. ENVY

Envy is the last of the seven sins but by no means the least dangerous. It makes you hate yourself and everything about your life. It makes you disregard or resent what you have and are, and wish for something another has or is.

This was the first sin that attacked me. I wanted the kind of mom Mark had, which caused me to hate my own mother and despise her. I couldn't focus on my life; I could only see the life I wanted that someone else had. So, there was no hope of satisfaction.

Envy destroyed my life. It sneaks in, so be intentionally grateful to prevent it before it can.

Innocence of God

How could God be innocent?

My whole life, I had longed to be innocent again—to be able to see the world as a child without worrying about the struggles of life, to know that my parents would handle my needs and problems. This is what God desires of us.

God doesn't hide behind cheap tricks to get you to follow Him. He speaks truth and offers His protection as a good Father; whereas, the devil lies and tricks man into following him, which leads to stress, worry and shame. We weren't meant for that. We were meant to live innocently in the loving arms of God with no worries and no cares.

No Worries

If I went into the middle of the desert with no food, no form of shelter, and no tools to use for my survival, I know God could keep me alive. God demonstrated His care for even the most insignificant things in the Gospel according to Matthew.

Look at the birds in the air; they do not sow or reap or store away in barns, and yet your heavenly Father feeds them. Are you not much more valuable than they?

Matthew 6:26

In this, we see God's provision and the fruitlessness of worry. The Lord is with you today, and He won't abandon you tomorrow. Your security transcends your circumstances. God desires for us to put our faith in Him, and, when we put our faith in Him, our worries fade away.

As we look into the eyes of the Father, everything else shifts into our peripheral vision. Like a racehorse with blinders, we too should have blinders that allow us to look at nothing else but the race before us and the Father in front of us.

Cast all your anxiety on him because he cares for you.

1 Peter 5:7

Have faith not only in His existence but in His desire for your greatest good. It's no coincidence that your reading this book, and there is no coincidence that exists within your life. All people and situations have a purpose. If not, then this really is a hopeless place. It's time we started looking at other people, ourselves and our situations through the eyes of God.

I no longer believe in coincidences. I think everything our senses detect has a purpose in the moment and in the trajectory of things. Everything is under the sovereignty of God and will give us a deeper understanding of Him if we look for it. Creation and all things in it already acknowledge Him.

The Lord is a rock that will not fail and will not leave. Reminders of His presence are everywhere. So many people try to suppress the love, the beauty and the order all around us; it can be suppressed, but if you want to find God, He will be found. If you want to lay down your worry, He will take it.

Solid Like a Rock

Time went on, and I started to realize the strength of our Lord. Even though I turned my back on Him, even though I was all alone—truly alone—He remained, like a solid rock.

> *The Lord is my rock, my fortress, and my savior; my God is my rock, in whom I find protection. He is my shield, the power that saves me, and my place of safety.*
>
> Psalm 18:2 (NLT)

In so many ways, God has been a rock to me. When all reality was shifting and melting away into nothing, God remained. God was the only thing within that lie I was told that could not be reasoned away. I could reason away all things in existence, but I could not reason away the creator of my existence. In this way, and many more, He is like a rock, unmovable and unshakable. Through all the millennia, He has been and will be here.

The things I went through, help me to live for Him as I do now. They help me to believe in Christ and trust that we have the ability to do all things through Him (Phil. 4:13). The Father walks with me in the darkest of valleys (Psalm 23) and in the highest of mountains. When everyone leaves me, He is there.

When I embraced Christ, I could love again. It felt weird not loving the things of the world at first, but there is no revelation more beautiful than God's love.

The Gospel

What is the Gospel?

I had always heard *about* the Gospel, but I never heard the Gospel. So, I have decided to include it within this book.

Who is Jesus? How is He the Savior of the World?

God the Father is a God of love, mercy, and justice. Man is a selfish creature made by God that desires to do nothing more than worship his own image or achievements. Man deserves nothing more than the wrath and justice of God. All men have committed sin in the eyes of God. Sin being anything that glorifies, extols or elevates man higher than his creator. Sin is any and every moral failure. It is disobedience of God's law.

> *Everyone who sins breaks the law; in fact, sin is lawlessness.*
>
> 1 John 3:4

What is God's Desire?

Sin is a rebellious choice against the will of God. A choice that every man has made and is held responsible for making. Thus, all of mankind is deserving of the justice of God. All man deserves to be sent to hell, no matter how "good" his life appears to be, no matter the amount of good deeds done. Disobedience to law cries out for justice; yet, God desires mercy for all of His creation. Both justice and mercy flow from God's love.

Say to them, 'As surely as I live, declares the Sovereign Lord, I take no pleasure in the death of the wicked, but rather that they turn from their ways and live. Turn! Turn from your evil ways! Why will you die, people of Israel?'

Ezekiel 33:11

How is God Loving and Just?

It is loving for God to be just, for it is just for God to be loving. Justice and love work in tandem with each other for the good of man. You cannot have justice without love, nor can you have love without justice, they are intertwined.

Even man can look at justice and see that justice is fair. The penalty fits the crime. To disobey God is not only choosing yourself over another, disobedience is the claim to be higher than another. To disobey God is the claim to be higher than God Himself. Claiming to be higher than God, to not need God, or that He (your creator) has no power over you, deserves the only penalty God can assign, the absence of Himself. God is life, and life is from God. Every breath, blink, smell, step, word and action is only possible through God. He permits man to live. He permits man to sin.

Though man is worthy of being cut from the One who gives life, God desires mercy. This is where Jesus comes in.

What Does Following Jesus Do?

When we follow Jesus, God sees the innocence of Jesus covering us instead of our constant tarnishing sins. Through Jesus, God's justice is appeased, allowing man to come under His mercy,

> *Yet the Lord longs to be **gracious** to you;*
> > *therefore he will rise up to show you **compassion**. For*
> *the Lord is a God of **justice**.*
> > *Blessed are all who wait for him!*
>
> Isaiah 30:18 (bolded words mine)

It is only through faith in Jesus and His ability to atone for man's sins and God's cosmic justice, that man receives the mercy of God.

Faith in Christ leads to following. Following leads to the cross. And, the cross that leads to resurrection.

Through Jesus, sin's need for justice is atoned. Jesus, the God-man who walked this earth without sinning, was able to appease the justice of the Father, so that the Father could remain just. And, by remaining just, He could remain loving. Jesus, the God-man that was beaten with sticks He created, cursed by those whose breath He gave and killed by the people He loved died on a wooden cross in 33 AD so that man might be right standing through His atoning death. And not just right standing, but resurrected to live with the Father for eternity, just as Jesus was resurrected three days after His atoning sacrifice on the cross.

> *He who did not spare his own Son, but gave him up for us all—*
> *how will he not also, along with him, graciously give us all things?*
>
> Romans 8:32

How Do I Follow Jesus?

Repent from Sin. Allow God into your life. Be honest with Him, even if that means telling Him you don't feel ready to follow Him. Ask Him to show you how to be obedient to Him.

Throw away all your old ways. Count them as loss. Cry out to God for mercy. Seek nothing but Jesus.

> *I urge you, brothers and sisters, in view of God's mercy, to offer your bodies as a living sacrifice, holy and pleasing to God—this is your true and proper worship.*

Romans 12:1-2

> *Then he said to them all: "Whoever wants to be my disciple must deny themselves and take up their cross daily and follow me.*

Luke 9:23

> *Whoever finds their life will lose it, and whoever loses their life for my sake will find it.*

Matthew 10:39

O soul are you weary and troubled?
No light in the darkness you see?
There's light for a look at the Savior
And life more abundant and free.

Turn your eyes upon Jesus.
Look full in His wonderful face.
And the things of earth will grow strangely dim
In the light of His glory and grace.

Through death into life everlasting
He passed, and we follow Him there.
Over us sin no more hath dominion.
For more than conquerors we are.

His word shall not fail you, He promised.
Believe Him and all will be well.
Then go to a world that is dying
His perfect salvation to tell.

-    *Hellen Howard Lemmel*

Part IV

Part V
Life With God

Now What?

So, what's the point? I unintentionally tested God, and He brought me back. Now what? Life is easy? Not so much. My tripping days were over but not forgotten.

As you probably noticed, I was mentally *stuck* in my first trip long after it concluded. Though I believed in God and the devil, I didn't necessarily believe everyone and everything around me was real. It was a struggle. All my thoughts since then have come under attack. I've questioned every detail of creation and existence, and the devil's used this weakness to undermine my quest for truth.

Trips made my mind vulnerable to direct interactions with demonic forces—encounters and exchanges that affected my life forever. Even the reality of those times that I encountered strange demonic forces, the demons called into question. making me second guess my own personal experiences and questioning my own senses, even the breath I felt on the back of my neck. Drugs are the devil's playground.

The breath I felt on the back of my neck during second trip was notably different than all of the other exchanges. Everything else filled me with terror, but the breath was warm. Instead of freaking me out, it calmed me and gave me peace. I learned later the Bible talks about the breath of God.

> *The Spirit of God has made me; the breath of the Almighty gives me life.*
>
> *Job 33:4 (underlined words mine)*

I believe God breathed on me that day. What grace He has shown me. It was an invitation to a new life, a life that had been given to me by Him.

If you are lost and alone, call on Him and offer all that you are. If you desire to be in God's presence, seek Him. If that seems impossible, ask Him to help you. He wants you to know Him.

The Process of New Life

It took a while to feel like I had strength after that second trip. I didn't go to many places. I mainly just walked around the house, sometimes going outside to appreciate the beauty of the world. I had no friends and didn't desire any.

It's hard to pick up where you left off after so long on drugs. For years, I hadn't eaten on a normal schedule. I didn't even remember what food tasted like without being high. Crazy, right?

I went back to work at the same place, with the same people, but I felt God tell me to put in my two weeks' notice. That threw me a little. *What will I do now?* I wondered. Still, I knew God would provide.

So, for a time, I had nothing to do except love a God who I had only begun believing in—It was kind of like a honeymoon. It didn't feel forced like it did when I was a kid. I had a genuine appetite for God, and I just wanted to love Him with everything I had.

I used this time to focus on getting my life back on track and listen for God. Fears still plagued me, and the nightlight I hadn't needed since I was three came back into play. At times, thoughts of my old friends returned, but this time, they came with sorrow because I knew of the deception they were still under. I regretted a lot of the choices I made during this time, including the lies I told that lured Mark into weed.

Frequency Change

A few days later, I got back in the car for the first time. As soon as I turned it on, the radio played blaring static on a frequency I'd never used before. I remembered the voices that came so clearly from the radio the last time I was in the car. Freaked out, I turned it off. Then, I sensed the voice of God telling me not to fear, that the voices will not harm me when I am with Him. I felt Him telling me to turn the radio back on to a normal station.

Every song I heard that day, I had never heard before in my life. They weren't Christian songs, but every one of them was a testimony of God's love. I don't remember them exactly, but one was about being able to do anything when *we* are together, another sang of how incredible *he* is.

Even the commercials amazed me. They were all parables of God.

I thought back to the message from my first trip: All things tell you you're in a box, and you can't understand them. But, in reality, everything was singing the praises of God, telling me God is good, and He is with me.

As I drove I cried tears of joy and gratitude. I never put another rap CD in my car. I just stuck with radio. And, without fail, every time, no matter the station, the songs poured out messages of God's love.

Yeah, it's strange. It was amazing. And, that experience helped me make sense of verses like this one in the Gospel according to Mark.

> *The secret of the kingdom of God has been given to you. But to those on the outside everything is said in parables so that, they may be ever seeing but never perceiving, and ever hearing but never understanding.*

Mark 4:11-13

God showed me His love in other ways as well. Each one was a gift. Pray and ask God to show Himself to you.

Max

Remember during the second trip when I told my cat to guard the door? I simply said that as a joke but something strange happened there, too. The cat, which had always slept in my sister Michall's room, now positioned himself at the front door each night, just staring, as if he was guarding it. I didn't notice the behavior change right away, but one night, I happened to glance at the cat who was staring at the door, and the memory of that night came rushing back. He stared at that door every night for 4 years, until the day he died. Now, I'm not saying the cat was actually guarding the door, but at the very least, it was a constant reminder of God's protection.

How great is God that He keeps me secure in His arms. As I recovered, I realized what if felt like to remember again. On drugs, it was like the previous day never existed. New memories resurfaced every day, and I could see them with new eyes. I could see them as opportunities God provided for my escape—opportunities I squandered. *How could I be so blind?* I thought. When we forget about God, He doesn't forget about us.

Vacation

About a week later, my parents decided we'd all head down to the beach in Corpus Christi—just a few hours away. Some friends allowed us to stay in their summer home for a couple of nights.

I think God was preparing me to face new temptations. I heard God tell me that in Corpus I would be tempted. I didn't have the desire to smoke, and I hadn't even thought about it for over a week, but when we arrived at the beach, I fell the first temptation that came my way.

I thought, *Everything in moderation, right? It's vacation. It's okay to relax a bit.*

Our first night there, I heard rock music coming from somewhere along the beach. I told my parents "I'm going to go find out where the music is coming from." I left my family and walked all the way to a stage where I found a band playing live. It must have been around 10:30 PM, and everyone there was very drunk. The band was wrapping up, and wouldn't you know? As I turned to leave, I heard someone calling my name.

"Keenan!" I heard a voice shout. I turned around and was blown away to see an old friend of mine from my town. He had a full bottle of Everclear vodka, and he handed it to me.

I knew this wasn't a coincidence, I knew it was a trap. But I thought, *Everything in moderation.*

"Here, have a drink, man," he said. And, I did. I didn't chug it, but I took a swig and got the kid's number (which might have been worse). I made plans to hang out with him the next day instead of with
my family.

I ended up hanging with my friend the whole time trip—what a waste. We drank the whole time, and not once did I have a good time. I wasn't listening to that new voice I had become acquainted with; I couldn't. God's voice was drowned out by my *moderation.*

On the last day at the beach, I found out another friend of ours, Matt, was having a birthday the next day back in Austin. I decided to buy him some weed for the occasion. See where this is going?

So, I found a dude who sold weed—well, actually, he found me (funny how that happens). I kept thinking, *Everything in moderation.* And this wasn't any standard weed; it was the best tasting, best looking weed I had ever seen, ever. He even threw in a gram of hash for free (condensed weed, which at the time would have costed around $120 for a gram). I couldn't believe it. *Matt will be stoked,* I thought.

The Birthday Party

Matt's party started out normal. I saw a lot of old friends, like David, Matt, Creed, Jax, Ben and a few others. Of the ten people there, four were dealers. I handed Matt the birthday weed and started packing hash in the pipe.

I took one puff, and it hit me hard after having not smoked for such a long time. I noticed weird things taking place, like this back room that the dealers kept going in and out of, acting almost concerned. Loud thuds came from that back room even when none of them were in there, like something or someone was back there.

This room was blocked by a red curtain, which I caught a glimpse beyond for a moment, as someone let the curtain fall behind them after walking out.

"Hey, close that curtain!" one of the dealers yelled right when I saw a shadow cross the opening. Ty (one of the dealers), who was closest to it, reached for it quickly and pulled it completely closed, but I knew what I saw. Something dark and sinister lurked in that back room. Whether or not anyone else could see it, I could. I could sense it, as if I were in the presence of that same demonic thing I saw with Sky.

I sat down and thought about the fight between good and evil, the fight for mankind. Everyone around me was stoned out of their minds. I thought how I used to be one of those people who let my life pass me by while I got high. But now I had been given the gift to recognize, at least in part, the value of time. It's precious. The Lord gives each of us time to find our way, but when the devil causes a person to trade time for pleasure, he wins.

And that's what all drugs do—they steal your time. Instead of moving forward in life, a person cycles through highs and pursuits of highs. Don't let the devil steal your time.

Be very careful, then, how you live—not as unwise but as wise, making the most of every opportunity, because the days are evil.

Ephesians 5:15-16

The Sovereign Lord has opened my ears; I have not been rebellious, I have not turned away. I offered my back to those who beat me, my cheeks to those who pulled out my beard; I did not hide my face from mocking and spitting. Because the Sovereign Lord helps me, I will not be disgraced. Therefore have I set my face like flint, and I know I will not be put to shame.

Isaiah 50:5-7

As I looked around the room, it seemed these people were under a spell they couldn't escape, waiting for the pipe. I had already split from drugs, but this relapse experience sealed my decision. My mind was set like flint against drugs from that point on. Of course, that's when a new pressure came along.

A dealer busted out a bong to smoke some hash oil out of it (another form of weed). He passed the bong to David, who was already super high. David said, "I can't finish this. Keenan, you gotta hit this." God told me to say no, and I did. "Man, you're letting me down," David said.

People crowded around at that point. One of them said, "Don't be such a bitch. Hit the damn bong," but I wouldn't. Finally, David, who was freaking me out at this point, said, "Mark, you want to hit this?" My heart sank. *Why did I even get Mark into this years ago? I led him into a trap,* I thought. Mark was thrilled to hit it.

I had pulled Mark into this world with lies, and I didn't know the way out. To be honest, I still don't know any way besides God to truly get out of the grips of that life. God saved me, and He will save anyone who calls on His name. I told Mark, "Don't hit it," but he just called me a pussy.

I hadn't driven myself to this party, so I had to wait around for Creed before I could leave. I heard the sounds of people playing beer pong behind me and them saying, "Hahaha, what a bitch. Why don't you just kill yourself. You can end it all, you know." It was the same demonic message of death I had gotten on my trip.

Trying to escape the people talking behind me, I stepped onto the balcony and had a cigarette. I borrowed a lighter from my friend Zack, who was more like an acquaintance, and he ended up following me outside. I lit up, and in a strange voice, Zack said, "Where you been man? I've been missing you." Zack and I had never been good friends, so this sounded out of place. When I looked up at him, fear came over me. Light shined from behind his face, I could only see the lit-up edges of Zack's face. His voice and image in the light struck a chord within me, and I knew *what* I was talking to. This was the same scenario I had been in on those two fateful acid trips.

"Oh, just taking it easy. Staying at home," I said looking down as fear began to take hold of me.

"Why'd you cut your hair? You know changing your appearance doesn't change who you are, right?" Zack asked. (I had buzzed my hair two days after I got saved, so every time I ran my hand over my head I would be reminded that God was with me.) That was it for me—I knew I wasn't talking to Zack. I put my cigarette out and started to head back inside.

Zack blocked my way, "Aren't you gonna answer?" he demanded.

I couldn't look him in the eye. I wasn't speaking to Zack—I knew I was speaking to a demonic presence.

"What?" I said, making up an excuse. "Sorry, I forgot the question. Sorry, I'm stoned, dude. I need to go inside." He laughed a laugh that shot shivers down my spine and stepped aside.

Inside, a dubstep song came on with only one lyric, "Hail Satan," like a declaration, then the bass dropped. I walked straight to the iPod and changed the song, which made most of the people yell at me. I said, "Sorry, I really hate dubstep," and some of them agreed and decided to put other music on.

I went over to a wall and sat down against it. It felt good knowing no one was behind me. I started praying under my breath as I waited for Creed to decide to leave. As soon as I said the words, "Jesus Christ," three people in front of me laughed. "What's funny?" I asked.

"I don't know, we're high. Everything's funny," one of them responded.

Whether they knew it or not, it was the demons mocking the name of Jesus. There was a demonic presence all over that apartment. Eventually, Creed took me back to my family's house. It felt good to be back resting in the presence of God.

The Supernatural

I never knew the full extent of what was going on in that back room at Matt's party. I never knew why Sky ran at me that night we were tripping.

There's still a lot of mystery surrounding all of these events, but the running theme within them all is opportunity— opportunity to take God's way of escape from the grips of death or the opportunity to receive the devil's influence and let things like drugs possess you.

The people around us really do influence us, and some of them have walked a long way with the devil's influence. Be on guard. A trap can be as obvious as a man calling himself legion (Luke 8:26-39) or as subtle as friend handing you a joint.

> *For you were once in darkness, but now you are light in the Lord. Live as children of light (for the fruit of the light consists in all goodness, righteousness and truth) and find out what pleases the Lord. Have nothing to do with the fruitless deeds of darkness, but rather expose them.*
>
> Ephesians 5:8-11

> *For our struggle is not against flesh and blood, but against the rulers, against the authorities, against the powers of this dark world and against the spiritual forces of evil in the heavenly realms.*
>
> Ephesians 6:12

The Availability of Prayer

I didn't go back to hard drugs after that experience at Matt's. I did smoke, but I never experienced a high—only an awareness of the battle between good and evil—God and the devil. I felt exposed to demonic attack through the ones I surrounded myself with. I separated myself from all of those old friends except David, whom I found to be inspirational on lots of levels. He sold weed at the time, but he was a good man.

I always prayed for David to stop selling and find Christ. I prayed every day. Over the weeks of me praying over him, his customers dried up. He didn't know how he would pay his rent, so I began praying for that, too. He got a good job at an auto parts store. Though he still does not follow Christ, I still pray for him.

The Power of Prayer

Life had settled quite a bit since my conversion and subsequent relapses and repentance. Two weeks after vacation, I asked my dad, "That morning, when I was lying on the couch coming off that acid, what were you doing?" Like I mentioned before, there were loud fight sounds coming from my parents' room. I just had to find out.

"I was praying," he said.

"Really?" I said. "It sounded like you were fighting someone."

"No, I was just back in my room, kneeling down on my bed, praying for you," he repeated.

Prayer

Prayer *is* battle. Prayer is calling on the Father to battle against the principalities of Darkness that are constantly at work against us. I have already quoted Ephesians 6:12 twice, but it is undeniably true. Our *struggle* is against those who we cannot see, and is that really that hard to believe? The human eye cannot perceive sound waves, yet they are proven to exist. Why is it so hard to believe there is an entire spiritual world surrounding us that we have never seen? We live in the shadow of the real. In order to move a shadow, you would not try to move the shadow, you would move the object casting the shadow. This is the same relationship between our reality and the spiritual world. In order to see this world change, call on the one who casts this world into existence. But prayer isn't only battle, it's so much more than that. Prayer is communion with God. Prayer can be enjoying a sunset and giving God thanks. It can be dancing, enjoying food or talking with friends. Prayer happens anytime we deliberately focus on God and invite Him into our lives, conversations and being. Prayer is not only requesting things from God but being with God. Pray.

The Will of God

I started looking for a job, and I found three that sounded interesting. I really wanted to be a gas station clerk, and the gas station a couple blocks away was hiring. I eagerly drove to the station expecting to be hired on the spot—after all, I knew the creator of the universe. But when I returned with my application, the position had been filled. Disappointed, I prayed as I drove away, "Lord, if I'm not supposed to work there, let Your will be done. Please put me somewhere I enjoy." It is okay to ask for what you desire as long as we don't base God's goodness on His *delivery*, like a candy machine. My faith in Him was unshaken. His existence and goodness are not based on His answer to prayer; they're based on the cross.

A week passed, and on my way to the skatepark, I stopped by a different gas station than the one I had applied. This was the gas station closest to the skatepark and was another one I wanted to work at. As the manager was ringing up my purchase, he made a comment about a worker that hadn't shown up. I offered to work at the gas station and was immediately hired. Isn't that a beautiful picture of the way God works as we seek Him faithfully, patiently, knowing that He is concerned with our greatest good?

God provided a job I loved, but I still had no friends. I had a deep desire to fellowship with someone, so I prayed about it. I asked for someone to come into my life the next day.

The very next day, my uncle came into town from Florida, and we ended up talking for *two hours* about the Lord. He said, "I don't really know why I came all the way here to Texas. I thought I was just going to pick up a motorcycle. But I truly believe this conversation is the real reason I came. Thank you, Keenan."

Doing Life with God

I still feared my room since the night I'd seen it filled with demons, so I had been sleeping on the couch since then. One day, when I was watching TV on the couch, the Lord spoke to me to grab my weapon (my Bible) and go to my room, because *we* were going to destroy a demon.

I couldn't bear to think of looking a demon in the eyes again. Scared, I grabbed my Bible and stared down the hall to my bedroom door. *I can't believe I'm about to do this,* I thought, as I took strength from the memory of running head-on at Sky.

As I started to walk toward my bedroom, my pace quickened almost to the point of a full-on sprint. I swung open the door expecting to come face to face with a demon. But instead, I saw my brother, swinging like a monkey in his hammock.

Laughter poured out of me, and I felt God say that conquering what we needed to conquer would be this easy as long as I was with Him, that nothing was impossible, and I needed to have courage. I smiled the rest of that day and started sleeping in my bed again.

One night, as I fell asleep, I wondered, *Lord, what about people in other countries? If you care so much, how could You let them worship another?*

The next morning, I heard the TV downstairs airing the news. The reporter said, "In the last few weeks, thousands of Muslims have reported visions of Jesus. Here are their stories."

I heard God tell me to reach those I have in front of me and to not worry about the rest, because He will care for the ones in front of me and the ones who are not. There is no person He cannot reach.

> *I revealed myself to those who did not ask for me; I was found by those who did not seek me. To a nation that did not call on my name, I said, 'Here am I, here am I.' All day long I have held out my hands to an obstinate people, who walk in ways not good, pursuing their own imaginations—a people who continually provoke me to my very face.*

Isaiah 65:1-3

Our God

God is amazing. He invites us to come into His home and bring others. Some ask, "If Jesus is God, why are there so many others?" We want excuses to ignore God. We feel the tug on our hearts to surrender, but things like fear and pride get in the way. We want to be our own gods, but we can't. It doesn't matter who a man calls "god," because God does not need man's approval to be God.

All people were made for a purpose wholly wrapped up in God. Fulfillment comes from complete submission, which is the way life was meant to be lived. This crosses cultures and economic statuses. This is the truth.

Life apart from God leaves people unsatisfied and unfulfilled. We are designed to embrace the life of God, and to worship at His feet. It is when we are worshipping Him that we receive the greatest gift of the universe—His love. Despite what we do, God loves his creation. When we worship Him, we reciprocate His love back to Him; thus, we partake in the love of God. Nothing is greater than being in the love of the Father and partaking in His glory.

The Last Story

For a short time after, I could hear spiritual messages through radio and TV broadcasts. I believe God was displaying his ability to do all that I saw the enemy do but with greater effect.

One day, I talked with Jax in my car as we waited for David to get off work. I hadn't seen Jax in months. I told him my long and crazy testimony—even the part about the radio. "Okay, here, listen," I said. I turned off the rap he had been playing and turned on the radio. A song came on and the lyrics said something along these lines, "Listen to these words of truth. Now is the time for change. Now is the time to listen."

Jax laughed, "I know all of what you have been talking about exists. I just choose to ignore it."

"Whether or not you ignore it makes no difference to the truth. God will not stop chasing you. Man runs out of breath in the sight of death. We cannot outrun God. The sooner we stop running, the sooner we experience the loving joy of the Father," I said. Jax shrugged and put his rap back on.

Prayer is such a powerful instrument. That's why I pray under my breath constantly. God does amazing things in response to His children's prayers. Both of my grandfathers had cancer at the same time. I prayed for both of them and received messages of their healing the next day—hallelujah! I prayed Mark would escape the pit I dragged him into, and he moved away and got away from those friends. I prayed God would separate so many of my friends who were taking each other further into darkness. Jax moved away for a bit and returned. God is still working on him.

Not all of my prayers are answered the way I ask or expect or hope. Many times, the answers totally surprise me in a way I didn't see coming.

I prayed Creed would get a job he loved and would be able to break away from his destructive lifestyle. Then, a fight separated Creed and Jax. Creed took a job at a local skate shop, and God has truly blessed him. I prayed that his 666 neck tattoo would get covered or removed. The devil has no right to claim that soul. After two years, he got it covered with another tattoo—in the shape of a cross, no less.

The list goes on and on. I could write a book just on answered prayers in my life, but why don't you experience the goodness of God for yourself? I pray for you, the reader, that God's love will fill and bless you. Amen.

Our Choice

Our time on earth is short and embroiled in a spiritual battle. We can't exit the war; we can only decide whose army conscription we fall under. God has given man the option of desertion from the ranks of His enemy through the sacrifice of His son Jesus.

> *Therefore God exalted him to the highest place and gave him the name that is above every name, that at the name of Jesus every knee should bow, in heaven and on earth and under the earth, and every tongue acknowledge that Jesus Christ is Lord, to the glory of God the Father.*

Philippians 2:9-11

Will your knee bow in resentment or humility? Shame or gratitude? Make no mistake—God has already won, but we are invited to share in that victory, becoming like Christ in the process. There is an enemy lurking in the darkness set on raising generations of rebellion. The choice of your master is your own.

Spiritual Attacks

The devil is an artist of war with tactics like music—a beautiful gift used to glorify the creator, perverted to glorify the creation. Everyone enjoys some kind of music, and it's a perfect carrier for overt and subliminal messages. A good beat draws a person to listen to a song, even one with lyrics the person thinks are bad. Over time, if the beat is good, you tell yourself the song is good and, consequently, you put your stamp of approval on the lyrics.

I fed my soul evil messages through music for a long time, and it was extremely ignorant of me. Pay attention to the messages coming to you from your daily surroundings—people, music, TV, games and all other media. Our eyes and ears are the gateway to the soul and must be guarded.

Everything you see, hear and touch either pulls you toward or away from God. Our senses and sentience can allow us to find, enjoy, and adore God with our whole being; yet, we use these gifts of God to indulge our flesh instead.

Life is much more than what exists in the physical world. God wants us to trust Him to meet our needs, whether we're starving for physical food or emotional connection—He is everything

Follow God and don't let the insanity of the world pull you away. There is nothing to gain in this world of any lasting value. You don't have to sift through your life judging, *Okay, is this right/wrong? Good/bad?* God—the embodiment of goodness—is judge. He judges righteously and will lead His followers in the paths of righteousness. Life blooms through obedience in Christ.

> *Seek first his kingdom and his righteousness, and all these things [eat, drink, clothing] will be given to you as well.*
>
> Matthew 6:33

Ask, and Ye Shall Receive

On drugs, I didn't worry about food, drink or clothing. So, was I righteously trusting God to meet those needs? No. I was content with my two pairs of pants, lack of transportation and empty wallet, but that satisfaction was fueled by distraction, not peace.

Now, I am grateful for what I have—big or small—and I'm not afraid to ask for the desires that rise up in my heart. Jesus talked about the power of asking in James and the Gospel according to John:

Verily, verily, I say unto you, whatsoever ye shall ask the Father in my name, He will give it to you. Hitherto ye have asked nothing in my name: ask, and ye shall receive, that your joy may be full.

John 16:23-24 (KJV)

When you ask, you do not receive, because you ask with wrong motives, that you may spend what you get on your pleasures.

James 4:3

First, ask for Christ. Only then will your motives and desires have a chance of being pure. To see the Lord answer prayers and move in life, we must first have Him in our lives.

Conclusion
God Is

Please give these final thoughts and the stories you've read up to this point some time to swirl around in your mind to form a conclusion.

My downfall began when I accepted a lie as truth. Soon after, my whole world was built on lies. Lies that used to serve my pleasures ultimately turned on me, transfixing me almost to the point of death. Then, God bombarded me with His goodness.

The experiences that led to my conversion were strong enough to make a longtime drug addict quit on the spot and write a book over the next five years. Was it real? Yes.

The demonic message to me said I was the only one who existed. But, you, the reader, also exist. You are on your own journey of faith, deciding where to go and who to put your faith in. You did not create yourself; nor did the first Adam create himself. You have a creator. And this is the crux of my argument.

If you are real then what I was led to believe is a contradiction, since, in this world, I am supposed to be the only one that exists. Your existence alone means that everything I was told is a lie. Your existence means that I was lied to by a power not of this world. This then means another world lives beyond the veil of the physical world we see. This other world must be one of two options:

1. It is simply a world like this one I live in, of which I am the entertainment or,
2. God exists and is constantly reaching out to humanity while battling against the devil, a battle in the middle of which I had been caught.

The deciding factor of these two options is the existence of the reader, the existence of you. If you are real, then so is my Lord God Jesus Christ. If you are not, then I guess I'll just live the rest of my multiple existences inside the cage of life.

Like he did for me, the devil will construct an elaborate lie just for you, catered to your every desire. And this lie will be beautiful. He'll offer you all the desires of your mortal self and hang you by them (just like he tried to do to Jesus in Luke 4, Matthew 4, Mark 1 and John 6). He will give you any false belief that will keep you out of the arms of the Father. But the devil's power and resources are limited and no match for God's. The devil's lies will only ever give a fraction of the fulfillment you were meant to have in the Lord, in Jesus.

Let God reveal His existence to you and lead you along the way of life in Christ—the only antidote to the devil's beautiful lie.

Made in the USA
Monee, IL
15 July 2020